Have You Eaten Grandma?

Gyles Daubeney Brandreth is an English theatre producer, actor, politician, journalist, author, and TV presenter. Born in Germany, he moved to London at the age of three and, after his education at New College, Oxford, he began his career in television.

He went from presenting *Puzzle Party* in the 1970s, to appearing in *Countdown*'s Dictionary Corner for over 300 episodes. His career has since encompassed becoming an MP and appearing regularly on TV and radio, but writing is his true passion.

His past books include; *Word Play*, *Oxford Dictionary of Humorous Quotations* and *Breaking the Code: Westminster Diaries*.

Have You Eaten Grandma?

GYLES BRANDRETH

MICHAEL JOSEPH
an imprint of
PENGUIN BOOKS

MICHAEL JOSEPH

UK | USA | Canada | Ireland | Australia
India | New Zealand | South Africa

Michael Joseph is part of the Penguin Random House group of companies
whose addresses can be found at global.penguinrandomhouse.com.

First published 2018
001

Copyright © Gyles Brandreth, 2018

The moral right of the author has been asserted

p.222 © Estate of Philip Larkin, with permission from Faber and Faber Ltd.

Every effort has been made to trace copyright holders and to obtain their permission
for the use of copyright material. The publisher apologizes for any errors or omissions
and would be grateful to be notified of any corrections that should be
incorporated in future editions of this book.

Set in 13.63/16.04 pt Garamond MT Std
Typeset by Jouve (UK), Milton Keynes
Printed and bound in Great Britain by Clays Ltd, Elcograf S.p.A.

A CIP catalogue record for this book is available from the British Library

HARDBACK ISBN: 978–0–241–35263–2
OM PAPERBACK ISBN: 978–0–241–35264–9

www.greenpenguin.co.uk

Penguin Random House is committed to a
sustainable future for our business, our readers
and our planet. This book is made from Forest
Stewardship Council® certified paper.

For Michèle
Come get it bae

Introduction
Language Is Power

Language is power and how we use it defines us.

Think of Winston Churchill. 'I have nothing to offer but blood, toil, tears and sweat.'

Think of John Prescott. 'It was a terrible flight. Thank God I'm back on *terra cotta*.'

Think of Donald Trump. 'I will be phenomenal to the women. I mean, I want to help women.'

Think of Kourtney Kardashian. 'You're acting like drunk slobkabobs.'

Language is also what makes us human. As the philosopher Bertrand Russell remarked: 'No matter how eloquently a dog may bark, he cannot tell you that his parents were poor but honest. Only language can do that.'

And since the way we use language tells the world so much about us, it's worth getting it right.

If we've not met before, let me introduce myself. My name is Gyles Brandreth and I'm a language obsessive and a punctuation perfectionist. (That doesn't mean to say I always get it right, but I always aim to.) My mother was a teacher; my father was a lawyer; they brought me up with a love of words. And they sent me to good schools. I was educated by teachers of English who knew their grammar and the value of it. As a child I read dictionaries at breakfast and asked for a copy of Fowler's *Modern English Usage* for my tenth birthday. I have loved word games all my life. When I was twenty-three, I founded the National Scrabble Championships. Since then, whether as a journalist or a broadcaster, an actor or a member of parliament, words have been central to my life. I am proud to be the longest-serving resident in *Countdown*'s Dictionary Corner on Channel 4, the host of BBC Radio 4's *Wordaholics*, a regular on *Just a Minute*, a reporter on *The One Show* on BBC1, and the Chancellor of the University of Chester. Words are my everything.

So: welcome to *Have You Eaten Grandma?* It's an informal guide to punctuation, spelling, and good English for the twenty-first century. In the pages that follow, with what my publishers assure me is 'a nice [that means precise as well as pleasing] mixture of good humour and authority', I aim to anatomise some of the linguistic horrors of our time, work out where we've been going wrong (and why), and come up with some tips and tricks to help show how, in future, we can make fewer (rather than 'less') mistakes. All right?

Is 'alright' all right? You'll find out right here.

The Queen's English

'Really? I thought she was German.'

The Queen is British, of course, though partly of German heritage. Her husband is British, too, though born in Greece and brought up in France and Germany. They both speak good English, as do their children and grandchildren. Because the sovereign is the head of state and traditional fount of honour and wisdom in the land, good 'correct' English has been called 'the Queen's English' (or 'the King's English') for at least six hundred years. Shakespeare used the phrase in his play *The Merry Wives of Windsor*. But to speak good English you don't have to sound like the Queen. Good English isn't about your accent: it's about your ability to communicate — clearly, effectively, and (when you want to) passionately.

I am passionate about the English language. It's the richest language in the world. It's our heritage — and our hope. All the research shows that the better the English you speak and write, the happier and more successful you will be. People with better English get better jobs because they write better CVs and communicate more effectively in interviews. People who punctuate poorly and spell badly are marked down in examinations — and in life. People with better English are more likely to secure the partner of their dreams because (the research shows) when it comes to wooing, words are more important than looks, money, or sex appeal. People with better English are healthier and live longer lives because they can understand and communicate better with doctors, nurses, and carers. Good English makes all the difference. And, alarmingly, good English is under threat.

In a recent survey, four out of five teachers expressed concern about the vocabulary range of their teenage pupils. Apparently, 'many are unable to understand questions in GCSE and SATs test papers, leading in some cases to low self-esteem'. Some eleven-year-olds did not know words such as 'complete', 'replace', and 'insert'. Some sixteen-year-olds struggled with 'explain', 'identify', and 'analyse'. Another survey revealed that while nine out of ten primary school children could identify a Dalek, only a third could recognise and name a magpie. The world is changing and words are disappearing. The majority of primary school children these days are city-dwellers and up to two-thirds of them, it seems, are unfamiliar with such lovely words as these:

acorn

bluebell

bramble

dandelion

heron

kingfisher

lark

newt

otter

raven

starling

willow

wren

YouTube, the video-sharing website owned by Google, recently asked two thousand people, aged from sixteen to sixty-five, their views on the current state of the English language. Ninety-four per cent thought there had been a decline in the correct use of English since the turn of the millennium, with four out of five identifying young people as the worst culprits. The same survey also found that three-quarters of adults now use emojis to communicate with one another. If a small digital image — designed by someone else and generated for you — can express how you feel, who needs words?

The explosion of social media in our time has had a discombobulating effect on the way we use language. President Donald Trump's preferred means of communication is the tweet and his favourite form of punctuation is the exclamation mark. Last year alone, in his tweets he used 3,660 of them! And as well as saying weird things in weird ways ('Sorry losers and haters, but my I.Q. is one of the highest — and you all know it! Please don't feel so stupid or insecure, it's not your fault'), the American president has come up with some weird words of his own. When on Twitter he declared 'We're going to win bigly', a new word was born. I thought he meant 'bigly' as in 'hugely' or 'ginormously' or even 'supercalifragilisticexpialidociously' — but no, 'bigly' was Trump's Twitter shorthand for 'big league'.

I am not against Twitter. I am on Twitter myself. (Do get in touch: you will find me @GylesB1.) And I know that Jack Dorsey, the boss of Twitter, takes his responsibilities seriously. He tweeted recently: 'We're committing Twitter to help increase the collective health, openness, and civility of public conversation, and to hold ourselves publicly accountable towards progress.' Unsurprisingly, that tweet earned him a Bad Grammar Award from a national magazine that cares about words and language, but Jack's heart is in the right place and he's worth $4.6 billion, so what does he care?

Trump invented 'bigly' in 2016. 'Supercalifragilisticexpialidocious' (the longest new word to gain worldwide currency in my lifetime) was popularised by the 1964 film, *Mary Poppins*. In 2018, 'Meet me at McDonald's' isn't an invitation: bizarrely, it's the name some young people have given a fashionable haircut that involves a closely shaven back and sides with an unruly mop on top. From Airbnb to Generation Z, via TTC ('Trying to Conceive') and ransomware (the malicious software that threatens a cyber-attack unless ransom is paid), barely a day goes by without a new word or phrase turning up.

Which new words are acceptable? Which aren't? It's a minefield, particularly when you add political correctness to the mix. Qantas, the Australian airline, has recently advised flight attendants to avoid using the terms 'husband' and 'wife' and 'mum' and 'dad' as 'they can reinforce the notion that everyone is in a heterosexual relationship and make many families feel excluded'. 'Slobkabobs' is in; 'mum' and 'dad' are out.

What to do?

Read on.

How to Use This Book

This is my guide to that minefield. When it comes to punctuation, spelling, and the use of English in today's world, I'm here to tell you what's right, what's wrong, when it matters, and when it doesn't.*

Punctuation is important, but the rules are changing. Spelling is important today in a way that it wasn't when Shakespeare was a boy. Grammar isn't set in stone. Once upon a time, to split an infinitive was wrong, wrong, wrong. Since the coming of *Star Trek* in 1966, when 'to boldly go where no man has gone before' was what the now-iconic TV series promised to do, we've all been at it. 'To actually get', 'to really want', 'to truly love', 'to just go' – *you* may not like them as turns of phrase, but take it from me: they are acceptable nowadays. End of.

And that's acceptable, too. 'End of' as a complete, two-word sentence has even appeared in *Hansard*, the official record of proceedings in the British parliament. In 2018, a minister of the crown finished an official statement with a definitive sign-off. 'End of,' he said, and sat down.

I'm a patron of the Queen's English Society — a charity that aims to keep the English language safe from per-ceived declining standards — but I'm not a dyed-in-the-wool traditionalist. I love the old, but I'm intrigued by the new. And sometimes excited by it, too. Looking at the English

---

* And, happily, following negotiations to rival those associated with Britain's departure from the European Union, I have persuaded my esteemed publishers to go along with me — even when the law I am laying down is at variance with their long-established in-house rules. For example, they stipulate the use of '-ize' endings in British English when I prefer '-ise'. They have let me have my way. And when it comes to the spaces around en dashes and ellipses, they made a bit of a fuss — and then caved in …

language today is like looking out over the city of London from the top of Big Ben. Spread below you, you will see old buildings that have stood the test of time and have a beauty and grandeur that lift the spirit. And alongside them, often dwarfing them, you will see new buildings, too, and you will think that some of them are striking and inspiring, and that some are monstrously ugly and should never have been put up in the first place. The landscape of the English language is much the same.

The Language of Grammar

'I'd like to see your mother, Alice,' said the teacher
when Alice opened the door.
'She ain't here, miss,' Alice replied.
'Why, Alice, where's your grammar?'
the teacher asked.
'She ain't here neither, miss,' said Alice.

To me, punctuation matters and good spelling is essential. Clear written communication depends on them. The words we use and the way in which we use them are fundamental, but the nuts and bolts of grammar — and the vocabulary of the grammarian — are less important to me. There are quite a few grammatical terms lurking in the pages ahead, but don't let them unnerve you. Coming up we have 'nouns', 'verbs', 'adjectives', 'adverbs', 'participles' (words formed from verbs, like 'going' or 'gone'), 'adjectival compounds' (aaargh!) and more besides. I have provided a brief guide to the language of grammar at the back of the book. Refer to it if you come across a term with which you are not familiar, but you don't need to understand all the intricacies of English grammar to be able to communicate well. I use a computer, but I have no idea how it works. I have a wife, but I have no idea why she stays. I take statins, and while the doctor did explain that they inhibit the HMG-CoA reductase — that rate-limiting enzyme of the mevalonate pathway — all I need to know is that they should help lower my bad cholesterol and reduce the risk of a heart attack.

This book can change your life. For the better. Enjoy.

There is no such thing as 'the Queen's English'.
The property has gone into the hands of a joint stock
company and we own the bulk of the shares!
Mark Twain

In my sentences I go where no man has gone before.
George W. Bush

The English language has a deceptive air of simplicity:
so have some little frocks; but they are not the kind that
any fool can run up in half an hour with a machine.
Dorothy L. Sayers

If you've got something you want to rap about,
just rap about it, man.
Yelawolf

1. Have You Eaten Grandma?

Good question. And one you could legitimately ask of your brother, your sister, or any of your first cousins, should you suspect them of being cannibalistically inclined.

I once met a lovely man who told me, with pride and a happy smile on his face, that he had eaten his grandma. And his grandpa, too. He belonged to the Gadaba people who live in the Indian states of Odisha and Andhra Pradesh. He explained that it is a Gadaba tradition to absorb the best of your grandparents' generation by eating them as soon as you can after they have died. It isn't as grisly as it sounds. First, you feed your dear departed to the fish in the local river, and then you eat the fish.

Of course, the enquiry you are intending to make may have nothing to do with tucking in to a female forebear. If, in fact, all you are wanting to find out is if your dear old gran has had her tea yet, the question is: 'Have you eaten, Grandma?' That comma after the third word is what makes the question mean what you want it to mean.

Punctuation — implied when we speak and written when we write — is an essential tool in communication. You can't make sense without it — *viz*[1] these horrors, each one of which I have seen in a public place.

---

[1] For some reason, English obsessives like me have a *penchant* for foreign phrases and abbreviations — e.g. **viz.** (or **viz** without a full

On a magazine cover:
Rachel Ray finds inspiration in cooking her
family and her dog

At a bus station:
TOILETS
ONLY
FOR
DISABLED
PREGNANT
CHILDREN

On a school computer:
We're going to learn to cut and paste kids!

In a country park in New York State:
HUNTERS
PLEASE USE CAUTION WHEN HUNTING
PEDESTRIANS
USING WALK TRAIL

---

stop, both are acceptable), short for the Latin ***videlicet***, meaning 'it is permitted to see', which is used as a synonym for 'that is to say' or 'as follows'. Usually it is used to introduce examples or further details to illustrate a point — as here. How do we get *viz* from *videlicet*? Another good question. Short answer: the abbreviation comes from a system of Latin shorthand developed around the year 63 BC that combined the first two letters of *videlicet*, *vi*, with the last two, *et*, when *et* in shorthand was indicated by a symbol that looks like our z. Get it? Got it? Good. I get this stuff from Stephen Fry.

12

At the local wildfowl and wetland centre:
QUIET
BIRDS HAVE EARS

In the street where I live:
GARAGE IN CONSTANT USE
ILLEGALLY
PARKED CARS WILL BE CLAMPED

In the street where my daughter lives:
SLOW
CHILDREN
CROSSING

These are signs of the times and symptomatic of the confusion that comes to the world when proper punctuation is neglected.

Punctuation is essential to clear communication. Without punctuation no one knows what's going on. When you are expressing yourself out loud, without perhaps realising it, the way you phrase what you are saying implies the punctuation you are using. A definite pause is a full stop — or 'period' to use the American term. An upward inflection is a question mark. A full-volume 'No!' accompanied by a look of disgust mingled with contempt and we can all hear an exclamation mark, if not several.

When you are expressing yourself on the page or computer screen, to make your intentions clear, to avoid ambiguity and confusion, you need punctuation. And the good news is: there are only a dozen or so punctuation marks and mastering their correct usage is a doddle. I'll start with the easiest and then move on ... [Those three dots — that's an ellipsis, by the way. It's annoying they don't just call them 'three dots', but they don't. And this is in square brackets rather than round ones for a reason. As you'll discover.]

The Full Stop or Period

This is what it looks like:

●

And you already know what it does. It ends a sentence and provides a definite pause.

In texts and tweets and even emails some people seem to think any punctuation unnecessary. Wrong. Yes of course you can write a brief message without punctuation it will probably be understood but its a bad habit to get into. (See what I did there?) It may take you marginally less time to write, but it will almost certainly take the intended recipient marginally longer to absorb. That is why, for example, in the age of the telegram, when you paid for each word used, senders were ready to pay to include the word STOP if it helped make their message more comprehensible.

Telegrams were telegraphic communications, originally sent by Morse Code, that when received by the telegraphic office were written or typed up in words and then delivered to the intended recipient by hand.

Enter Dr Hawley Harvey Crippen (1862–1910), the

American medicine man who was hanged for the murder of his wife having been the first suspect in criminal history to be captured with the aid of wireless telegraphy. The murder took place in London and Dr Crippen and his 'accomplice' were making their escape by sea, crossing the Atlantic to North America, when their ship's captain recognised them and sent this telegram to the British authorities:

HAVE STRONG SUSPICIONS THAT CRIPPEN LONDON CELLAR MURDERER AND ACCOMPLICE ARE AMONG SALOON PASSENGERS STOP MOUSTACHE TAKEN OFF GROWING BEARD STOP ACCOMPLICE DRESSED AS BOY STOP MANNER AND BUILD UNDOUBTEDLY A GIRL STOP

Pedants might like to have seen an extra STOP after MOUSTACHE TAKEN OFF, but no matter: the telegram did the trick. Dr Crippen was duly arrested, tried, and executed. Full stop.

In the United States of America, Western Union abandoned its telegram service in 2006. When I was in my twenties, and we still had a telegram service in the UK (it ended here in 1982), I sent them all the time. I worked in the theatre then and relished the extravagance involved in all those STOPs. 'When an actor has money,' said the Russian playwright Anton Chekhov, 'he doesn't send letters, he sends telegrams.'

In Russia, Japan, and Mexico they still have a telegram service, but in Europe it is only Italy that now maintains a tradition that you might have thought the text, tweet, and email had made redundant. Over the years probably the most famous telegram to come out of Italy was the one sent by the American journalist Robert Benchley to his editor at the *New Yorker*, Harold Ross, when Benchley arrived in Venice for the first time: 'STREETS FULL OF WATER STOP PLEASE ADVISE'.

Another of my telegram favourites was sent by the great American film director Billy Wilder in the mid-1950s when he was in Paris making a movie. It was at the time when the *bidet* was coming into fashion in the US as a must-have bathroom accessory and the then Mrs Wilder, back in Los Angeles, was determined to have one. She instructed her husband to buy her a *bidet* while he was filming in France and get it shipped over to Hollywood. Unfortunately, so great had been the recent demand for *bidets*, when Wilder went out in search of one he failed to find it. He wired his wife with the news: 'UNABLE OBTAIN BIDET STOP SUGGEST HEAD-STAND IN SHOWER STOP'.

In a nutshell, in contemporary written English full stops are used:

- to mark the end of a sentence that is a complete statement:
  You are reading my book. Thank you.

- to mark the end of a group of words that don't form a conventional sentence, so as to emphasize a statement:
  You are reading my book. My book. Wow. Thank you.

- in some abbreviations, for example, *etc., e.g., Jan., Feb., a.m., p.m.*:

> *Gyles is including lots of asides, anecdotes, incidental stories, etc., that may not always be as amusing as he thinks.*

NB.[2] If an abbreviation with a full stop comes at the end of a sentence, you don't need to add another full stop:

> *He really loves his asides, anecdotes, incidental stories, etc. Bless.*

- in website and email addresses:
  www.gylesbrandreth.net

---

[2] 'NB' stands for *nota bene*, Latin for 'note well' and used as an abbreviation by English writers since the mid-seventeenth century. It is acceptable these days to write it as 'NB', 'Nb', 'nb', 'N.B.', or 'N.b.', but it is most commonly written as 'NB.' '*E.g.*' stands for *exempli gratia*, Latin for 'for example', and is usually written as 'e.g.', although *eg* without full stops is acceptable if it appears in italics. *Etc.* or *etc* or *&c.* is an abbreviation of the Latin *et cetera* and means 'and other similar things'. *A.m.* is the abbreviation for the Latin *ante meridiem*, meaning 'before midday'. *P.m.* stands for *post meridiem*, meaning 'after midday'. A lower case *m.,* standing for *meridies* meaning 'midday', is sometimes used to indicate noon — but not often. In good written English, *a.m./ p.m.* is reckoned better than *am/pm* and either is better than *AM/PM*. When *a.m.* or *p.m.* appear at the end of a sentence, there is no need to add an additional full stop. And, of course, since the abbreviations specify an hour's relation to midday, it is not necessary to use *morning, afternoon, evening, night,* or *o'clock* with them. Three hours after midday is '3.00 p.m.', or '1500 hours' if you are using the twenty-four-hour clock. To say it is '3.00 p.m. in the afternoon' is WRONG.

The full stop is the most fundamental of all the punctuation marks. Essentially, think of the full stop as the moment when you take a proper breath before moving on.

Many writers of note use a lot of full stops. To add urgency to their writing. And impact. This is the opening line of Ray Bradbury's novel *Fahrenheit 451*:

It was a pleasure to burn.

This is the beginning of the closing chapter of Charlotte Bronte's *Jane Eyre*:

Reader, I married him.

Ernest Hemingway loved a short sentence. He knew how to pack a punch. Allegedly, when challenged to conjure up a complete short story in just six words, he came up with this, in the process using a colon, a comma, and a full stop to considerable effect:

For sale: baby shoes, never worn.

Hemingway knew that writing well isn't easy. 'I write one page of masterpiece to ninety-one pages of shit,' he admitted to F. Scott Fitzgerald in 1934. 'I try to put the shit in the wastebasket.' No shit.

As a rule, shorter sentences are preferable to longer ones. But don't overdo it. Please. It can feel mannered. And be irritating.

The opposite is quite as true. With an overlong sentence, the reader is likely to get lost. Charles Dickens, Jane

Austen, Marcel Proust, and Vladimir Nabokov are celebrated for their long sentences. James Joyce was notorious for his. His 1922 novel, *Ulysses*, features a sentence that runs to 4,391 words. Jonathan Coe went three times better with his 2001 novel, *The Rotters' Club*, managing to conjure up a single sentence of 13,955 words. (You'll have to take that from me. I don't have the space to quote it.)

The Comma

This is what it looks like:

,

You remember the old riddle:

> Q. What's the difference between a cat and a comma?
> A. One has its claws at the end of its paws, and one is a pause at the end of a clause.

That tells you much that you need to know about the comma, but, maddeningly, not quite everything.

A comma marks a momentary pause between different parts of a sentence — like an almost unnoticeable intake of breath. Commas exist to make the meaning of sentences clear by grouping and separating words, phrases, and clauses.

Let's start with separating words.

Commas in Lists

Commas are used to separate items in a list:

> I packed my bag and in it I put my brush, my comb, my
> toothpaste, my teeth, my pyjamas, and my book.

In a list there is no requirement for a comma before the
'and', unless the sense requires it. Here it is probably helpful:

> The list of the great lovers of history should include
> Adam and Eve, Troilus and Cressida, Antony and
> Cleopatra, and Kermit and Miss Piggy.

Without that final comma, you leave open the possibility
that Antony and Cleopatra and Kermit and Miss Piggy
were part of some sort of time-travelling foursome.
    How many people am I talking about here — two or
four?

> I want to thank my parents, Charles and Alice.

If it's just two people, my parents who are called Charles
and Alice, one comma is sufficient. But if it's four — my
parents plus Charles and Alice — to make that clear you
need to add an extra comma to your list:

> I want to thank my parents, Charles, and Alice.

'Making it clear' — that's what it's all about. And that's
why some people — especially those who went to Oxford

University or who work for the Oxford University Press —
insist on having a comma before the word 'and' even in
the most straightforward list. This is known as the 'serial
comma' or the 'Oxford comma', and it's useful:

> My favourite flavours of drink are orange, lemon, rasp-
> berry, and lime and ginger. They used to be strawberry,
> apple, pear, lime, and ginger.

Without the Oxford comma, you can give people the
wrong idea. Famously, *The Times* newspaper once ran a
brief description of a television documentary featuring
Peter Ustinov, promising:

> Highlights of his global tour include encounters with
> Nelson Mandela, an 800-year-old demigod and a dildo
> collector.

You also use a comma to separate two or more adjectives
which are modifying a noun:

> He was a tall, dark, handsome, devilishly amusing man.

Here the commas are as good as standing in for the word
'and' and you could rephrase the sentence using the word 'and'
if you wanted to:

> He was a tall, dark, handsome and devilishly amusing man.

When you wouldn't use the word 'and', you don't need a
comma:

He was an outstanding British author.

As well as being used to separate items in a list, commas are used to separate phrases and clauses.

Getting Complex: Commas in Clauses

'Most of the time, travellers worry about their luggage' is both true and correctly punctuated. Lose that comma after the fourth word and suddenly we're in *Doctor Who* territory: 'Most of the time travellers worry about their luggage.'

You use commas to separate clauses in what the grammarians call 'complex sentences' — that is, sentences complicated by the fact that they contain a 'main clause' and one or more 'subordinate clauses'.

The main clause tells you the main thing: 'Travellers worry about their luggage.' The subordinate clause is exactly that — subordinate, giving you that little bit of extra information that's not quite so important: 'Most of the time'.

Here are two sentences: a simple sentence, immediately followed by a complex one:

My husband is dark and handsome. When it's dark, he's handsome.

In the second sentence, the complex one, 'he's handsome' is the main clause and 'When it's dark' is the subordinate clause. You need to use a comma to separate the two.

Here are some more sentences where the comma is simply there to be a pause at the end of a clause:

I don't make mistakes, I marry them.

When it comes to charity, a lot of people stop at nothing.

You can have brains or beauty, but you can't have all three.

However...

So far, so easy. It gets more complicated, however, when the word 'however' comes into play. You must always use a comma after the word 'however' when 'however' means 'by contrast' — as in:

However, it gets more complicated.

However, you must not use a comma after writing the word 'however' when 'however' means 'in whatever way' — as in:

However you look at it, this punctuation
business isn't easy.

Indeed, it isn't. 'However', 'indeed', and 'moreover' are three words that should be followed by a comma — in certain circumstances.

Relative Values

'After a good dinner,' said Oscar Wilde, 'one can forgive anybody, even one's own relations.'

If you can come to terms with relative clauses, you deserve a good dinner. A 'relative clause' is a special kind of subordinate clause.[3] With relative clauses, the use of commas is key.

A subordinate clause beginning with 'who', 'which', 'that', 'whom', or 'where' is known as a relative clause — e.g.:

> Gyles, who has a wife and three children, is a proud husband and father.

A pair of commas, placed at either end of the relative clause, separates extra, incidental material from the rest of the sentence. Remove the relative clause and the commas and the sentence still makes sense, although we learn less from it:

> Gyles is a proud husband and father.

Where the relative clause is providing inessential, if interesting, extra information, or is providing a comment or side-observation, the commas come into play. But if the relative clause is introducing information that is *essential* to the understanding of the sentence, the clause is called a 'restrictive relative clause' and is presented without commas — e.g.:

> Passengers who are travelling First Class will receive a complimentary beverage service.

The 'restrictive relative clause' is 'who are travelling first class'. Take out those words and the sentence tells a different story:

---

[3] Santa's helpers are subordinate Clauses — but that's a different matter. [Sorry.]

Passengers will receive a complimentary beverage service.

If you haven't the time (or will) to master the difference between main clauses, subordinate clauses, relative clauses, and restrictive relative clauses, worry not. Essentially, to decide whether you need to use one comma, or a pair of commas, or none at all, read what you are writing and see if it makes sense. The way you use the commas should give your sentence its correct meaning — *viz*:

The men, who were handsome, found partners.

There, the relative clause tells us that all the men were handsome and all found partners.

The men who were handsome found partners.

With this restrictive relative clause, without commas, we are discovering something quite different: here, *only* the men who were handsome found partners.

It's all about clarity of communication. Where you put in your comma, or don't, can totally change the meaning of what you want to say. It's clear what this means:

He liked Nigella, who cooked pasta better than Delia.

It's clear this next sentence means something else:

He liked Nigella, who cooked pasta, better than Delia.

Up the Conjunction

You need to use a comma to separate two independent clauses when they are linked by a coordinating conjunction — that's a word such as 'and' or 'but' or 'yet' or 'so' or 'or' or 'nor' — *viz*:

People often accuse me of lying, but you don't
have to believe me.

She was determined to liven up the local library, so she
hid all the books on anger management.

Haikus are easy,
Yet sometimes they don't make sense.
Refrigerator.

A Quick Aside

Commas are used, too, to separate a part of a sentence that is an aside — a parenthetical phrase like 'naturally' or 'of course':

My short attention span irritates me, of course,
but not for long.

Don't use commas too frequently, but do use them:

- when you want your reader to pause:
  Do concentrate on this, please.

- when you want to give emphasis to an adverb:
    I am saying this, loudly, so that you take it on board
    is stronger than
    I am saying this loudly so that you take it on board.

- when you decide to omit a word to add drama to what you are saying:
    The night was young, his hopes were high.
    The dawn had arrived, his hopes were dashed.

- either side of the word 'too' when you are using the word 'too' to mean 'also'. And if the word 'too' comes at the end of your sentence, you should precede it with a comma:
    And her mother came, too. As ever, she was too ridiculous for words.

OMG, I Forgot the Comma!

Commas commonly come immediately after an interjection — *viz*:

Wow, you look pretty.

Uh-oh, have I gone too far?

Oh, forget it.

And if you are addressing someone by name, put a comma before the name to avoid confusion.
This is clear:

I fancy your sister, Basil.

You are talking to Basil and you've got the hots for his sister. This, on the other hand, is confusing:

I fancy your sister Basil.

What's happening? Is your sister called Basil? Or has a nun suddenly entered the equation? (Nuns can go by the names of male saints, as I'm sure you know.)

Use commas either side of information in a sentence that defines or modifies the name:

Donald's eldest daughter, Ivanka Trump, is a bit special.
Ivanka, daughter of the President and his first wife,
came to tea on Tuesday.

Don't use commas either side of a name unless the information in the sentence is specific to only that person. There's no need of them here:

My friend Ivanka Trump is a bit special.

Commas in Conversation

When you are reporting a conversation in writing, this is known as 'direct speech' and a comma is required after you have said who is speaking, with the comma coming before the first quotation mark:

Gyles said, 'Easy-peasy.'

*

28

You also need to use a comma at the end of a piece of direct speech, if the speech comes before the information about who is speaking — and here the comma goes inside the second quotation mark:

'Easy-peasy,' said Gyles.
'Bollocks,' they replied.

Inevitably, there are a couple of exceptions to this rule. If the piece of direct speech takes the form of a question or an exclamation, you end it with a question mark or an exclamation mark, and not with a comma:

'Bollocks!' they shouted, even louder than before.
'What are they saying?' asked Gyles.

When direct speech is broken up by the information about who is speaking, you need a comma to end the first piece of speech (inside the quotation mark) and another comma before the second piece (before the quotation mark):

'Yes,' Gyles admitted, 'commas can be challenging.'
'Challenging,' they responded, 'is not the word
we'd use.'

The Final Don't and Do

DON'T use commas to link main clauses that should be linked by conjunctions, or could reasonably stand alone as independent sentences, or could more suitably be separated by other forms of punctuation.

This sort of thing is not good:

> It was a sunny day, I went shopping,
> there were bargains galore.

This sort of thing is fine:

> It was a sunny day, so I went shopping.
> There were bargains galore.

This works, too:

> It was a sunny day; I went shopping;
> there were bargains galore.

(Yes, the semi-colon has its uses, as we're about to discover. Exciting.)

DO use a comma if it makes sense to do so. This, for example, is confusing:

> If you want to marry the vicar is the man you need.

This isn't:

> If you want to marry, the vicar is the man you need.

Think before you place your comma. Beginning an email like this is fine:

> Hi Gyles,

Beginning it like this is sinister:

Hi, Gyles,

Beginning it like this suggests not so much a greeting as a reprimand:

Hi, Gyles.

Remember the wise words of Sir Ernest Gowers (1880–1966), civil servant turned style guru, and author of the magisterial *Complete Plain Words* (1954): 'The use of commas cannot be learned by rule. Not only does conventional practice vary from period to period, but good writers of the same period differ among themselves ... The correct use of the comma — if there is such a thing as "correct" use — can only be acquired by common sense, observation and taste.' And, I might add, by reading what you have written out loud or in your head. You can tell where the comma should go, can't you?

PS.[4] Commas in Numbers

In Britain and the United States, we use commas to separate the digits within a number in groups of three — moving

---

[4] 'PS.' stands for *postscriptum*, Latin for 'written after', and can be written as 'PS' or 'PS.' or 'P.S.', but invariably in capital letters. The PS comes as an afterthought. The thought after that is the PPS, the *post-postscriptum*, and the one that follows is the PPPS, the *post-post-postscriptum*, and so on, *ad infinitum*. (And you guessed it: *ad infinitum* is Latin for 'to infinity'.)

from right to left if there is no decimal point, or, if there is a decimal point, from the decimal point to the left only:

> This is a million and one: 1,000,001
> This is just under a third of that: 333,333.666666
> And this is a millionth of that: 0.333333666666

To make life confusing (and to stir the spirit of diehard Brexiteers), in some countries, with their numbers, they use the comma and the full stop quite differently. In France, for example, '9.9' is written '9,9' and a million is written like this: '1.000.000'.

PPS. Billions and Billions

By the way, as numbers go, a billion is unique. It's a word for a number with two distinct definitions:

- In American English and modern British English a billion is one thousand million or 1,000,000,000.
- But historically, and officially up until 1974, the English billion was one million million or 1,000,000,000,000. We now call one million million 'a trillion'.

But mind how you go when you are buying your Bit-coins. Depending on the country you are in, a 'billion' might refer either to what we call a billion or to what we call a trillion. In a raft of European countries, they call a thousand million a 'milliard' and they call a million

million 'a billion'. (Yes, this is a book that can save you a fortune.)

The Semi-Colon

This won't take long; but it's important, believe me.

Read that sentence out loud and you should see exactly what the semi-colon is doing. It's providing a pause that is longer and more significant than a comma, and less abrupt and intrusive than a full stop.

The semi-colon looks like this:

;

And for those who relish nuance in their punctuation it's the go-to punctuation mark. I love the semi-colon; for my money, it's undervalued and underused.

I may be in a minority on this because many authors of note have written masterpieces without having recourse to the semi-colon. It's particularly eschewed by writers in the United States. According to Ben Macintyre, sometime London *Times* correspondent in New York and Washington, DC:

Americans have long regarded the semi-colon with suspicion, as a genteel, self-conscious, neither-one-thing-nor-the-other sort of punctuation mark, with neither the butchness of a full colon nor the flighty promiscuity of the comma. Hemingway and Chandler and Stephen King wouldn't be seen dead in a ditch with a semi-colon (though Truman Capote might). Real men, goes the unwritten rule of American punctuation, don't use semi-colons.

That's as may be; I beg to differ. The semi-colon is a subtle beast, and useful, too. What's more, it comes with a pedigree. First seen in print in 1494, the playwright Ben Jonson was the first English writer of significance to use it consistently, and Mark Twain, Edgar Allan Poe, and Herman Melville are among classic American authors who used it frequently and well.

The principal role of the semi-colon is to provide a break that is stronger than a comma, but not as final as a full stop. It should be used between two main clauses that balance each other — or contradict each other — but are too closely linked to be written as separate sentences:

I love my wife; she loves me.

I love my cat; my dog doesn't give a damn.

It should be used, too, when the second statement complements the first:

The cat has never been healthier;
the vet's bills can all be justified.

And in front of linking words such as 'however', 'never-theless', 'therefore', and 'besides':

> She hates the vet; however, the visits
> undoubtedly do her good.

Famously, the great P. G. Wodehouse aimed to avoid the semi-colon throughout his long writing life. I'm not sure how.[5] You *must* use a semi-colon when a comma is replacing a full stop in a quotation or a quotation is linking two separate sentences:

> 'I'm so sorry to have to tell you this,'
> he said; 'your cat has croaked.'

> 'Would you like her cremated?' his assistant enquired;
> 'we have a special offer this month.'

Semi-colons come in handy, too, with lists, when a comma alone is not up to the job. This is confusing:

> At the party we saw a stranger kissing the host, the host-ess, the stepson who appeared as high as a kite and a budgerigar that had escaped from its cage.

Commas in this instance simply can't deliver. Surely the stranger wasn't kissing the entire family? And was the

[5] Despite this, where I live we are Wodehouse devotees; for us, he is undeniably the master. My wife's favourite Wodehouse line comes from his novel *Mostly Sally*: 'And she's got brains enough for two, which is the exact quantity the girl who marries you will need.'

stepson as high as both a kite and a budgerigar? Here, only the much-maligned semi-colon can do the trick:

> At the party we saw a stranger kissing the host; the hostess; the stepson, who appeared as high as a kite; and a budgerigar that had escaped from its cage.

The Colon

The colon is the longest part of the large intestine, extending from the caecum to the rectum. *Oops!* Sorry: wrong book.

The punctuation mark known as the colon looks like this:

The word comes from the Latin word *colon*, meaning a limb or part of a limb, and, as a punctuation mark, has been around for more than four hundred years. In the old days it seems to have served as a kind of full stop with a second stop on top: a mark to indicate the need for a pause in a piece of writing. Now, its use is quite different. Look at the colon and think of it as a pair of binoculars placed vertically on the table. The binoculars will remind you of the colon's core purpose. It is there to help you look ahead. The colon does not separate or stop (like the comma, semi-colon, or full stop): it introduces what lies ahead: it takes you forward.

You use the colon for three principal tasks:

1. To introduce a list:

   Five people walk into a bar: an Englishman, an Irishman, a Scotsman, a bishop, and an actress.

2. To introduce direct speech:

   The barman asks: 'Is this some kind of a joke?'

3. To introduce an explanation or summary of the first part of the sentence or to take it further in some way:

   There are two problems with this joke: it is teetering on the edge of political incorrectness and it isn't funny.

When the colon is introducing a list, its role is straightforward:

   These are the first three months of the year: January, February, March.

When the colon is introducing direct speech, its use is optional: it can be replaced by a comma. Yes, this is acceptable:

   He asked: 'What are the first three months of the year?'

And so is this:

   He asked, 'What are the first three months of the year?'

What's not on is a mixture of the two:

> He asked: 'What are the first three months of the year?'
> She replied, 'Don't ask me.'

When it comes to introducing direct speech, in any one piece of writing decide whether you are going to use a colon or a comma and stick with it.

The third use of the colon is the one that's most fun. Essentially, it's there to introduce a summary/explanation/expansion of what's gone before:

> There is something to be said for procrastination: it ensures you've got something to do tomorrow.

But it can also be used to introduce the prospect of something that lies ahead:

> Spring was in the air: she might forgive him after all.

When you are unsure whether it's a colon or a semicolon that you need, remember those binoculars. If what follows the punctuation mark leads on from what precedes it, opt for the colon.

Colons have other uses, too:

- when telling the time, the colon can be used to separate hours from minutes, with no space before or after the colon:

    10:15 a.m.

- when expressing ratios of two numbers, the colon is used, again with no space before or after the colon:

  5:1

- with biblical references, the colon is used to separate chapter from verse, with no space before or after the colon:

  Proverbs 6:10[6]

- in correspondence in the United States, the colon is frequently used like this:

  Dear Mr Brandreth:
  Attention: Accounts Payable
  PS: You're fired!

- in the UK, we would present the above like so:

  Dear Mr Brandreth,
  Attention: Accounts Payable
  PS. You're fired!

In the UK, too, for more than two centuries, it was customary to follow the colon with a dash or hyphen, especially when introducing a list, like so:—

---

[6] As it happens, my favourite verse from the Bible: 'A little sleep, a little slumber, a little folding of the hands to rest, and poverty will come upon you like a vagabond and want like an armed man.' You have been warned.

Still to come: –
Dashes and hyphens,
Question and exclamation marks,
Brackets, asterisks, and apostrophes.

Nowadays, that unnecessary hyphen or dash is totally taboo. Don't be tempted to add it for old times' sake. It's simply not done any more. When it was used, the mark was known by typographers as 'the dog's bollocks', because of the way it looked. When you are picturing the colon, forget the dog's bollocks: stick with the binoculars.

(Since I have mentioned brackets, let me illustrate how they can be used with a brief parenthetical paragraph about 'the dog's bollocks' — a phrase that, as well as being the typographer's term for the colon-plus-dash, also means something outstanding or 'the best of its kind' and, as such, has been part of the English language for at least a century. 'Bollocks' as a word for testicles has been around for centuries. No one quite knows how 'the dog's bollocks' came to mean what it does — except perhaps, depending on the breed of dog, their bollocks can be outstanding and most dogs do seem to give them top attention. No one knows either who conjured up the 'pooch's privates' and the 'mutt's nuts' as synonyms for the dog's bollocks, nor which comedian first told us he loved North Korean cuisine: 'It's the dog's bollocks. Literally.')

Okay: time to move on.

2. Must Dash – Hyphen Can Wait

What's the difference between a dash and a hyphen? They look quite similar (a short dash and a hyphen are as good as identical) and they are often confused, but, in fact, in terms of what they do, they are quite different.

A hyphen joins two or more words (or parts of words) together, while a dash commonly separates words into parenthetical statements — or introduces a dash of something extra. Hyphens are not separated by spaces, while a dash (which comes in with two different and distinct lengths) usually has a space on either side of it.

Let's begin with the hyphen. The mark in the middle here is a hyphen:

non-stop

As it happens, when it comes to talking about hyphens, 'non-stop' is a good word with which to start. In French, when I say '*non*', I mean 'no'. In English, 'non' isn't a proper stand-alone word: it's a prefix — and one that pops up all over the place:

non-achieving
non-aggression

non-aligned
non-conformist
non-profit-making
non-speaking
non-stop
non-religious

But are those hyphens really necessary? 'Nonsense' doesn't have a hyphen in it, does it? Nor does 'nonentity'. And what about 'nonabsorbent'? Not sure about that one. How about you?

To hyphenate or not to hyphenate? That is the question. Is this correct:

The fair-haired non-smoking short-sighted chef was cooking a fry-up using a non-stick pan.

Or is this acceptable nowadays:

The fairhaired nonsmoking shortsighted chef was cooking a fryup using a nonstick pan.

Intriguingly, as I type this, my laptop (which was once a lap-top) is telling me that 'nonsmoking', 'nonstick' and 'shortsighted' are acceptable, but that 'fairhaired' and 'fryup' aren't. They should be 'fair-haired' and 'fry-up'. The truth is, the times they are achanging (or is that 'a-changing'?) and nobody (or is that 'no-body'?) quite knows.

Once upon a time, the hyphen was all-pervasive: now it's much less so. 'Cooperate' was 'co-operate'; 'prearrange' was 'pre-arrange'; 'email' was 'e-mail'. These days, especially in

America, the hyphen has fallen out of fashion big-time. (Should that have been 'bigtime'? Or 'big time'? Or 'Big Time'? You decide.)

I say 'You decide' not in a cavalier way (or out of coward-ice), but simply because the use of the hyphen is in flux and the old rules no longer apply. 'Cooperate' was once written as 'co-operate' because that's what made most sense of the word. Say 'cooperate' as it appears on the page and you might think the word had something to do with chickens or the folk who make barrels. Losing that hyphen wasn't helpful, in my view, but it's gone and that's that. I'm just hoping we don't lose the hyphen in 'co-owner', but quite soon we probably will.

The Brandreth Rule on hyphens is this: hyphenate when doing so will make the word easier to read, make more sense of it, or avoid ambiguity. Otherwise, don't.

- 'Nonstick' is easy to read, but 'notforprofit' isn't.
- A 'nonaggression pact' is acceptable, but a 'blueeyed hero' or a 'doeeyed girl' much less so.
- When you recover your old sofa from the skip and get it re-covered, it may take you a while to recover from the cost. (A hyphen can change the very meaning of a word.)
- No one uses 'no-one' any more, and no one should use 'noone', ever.
- Tim Cruise is a little-known artist; Tom Cruise is a little known actor.
- 'STUDENTS GET FIRST HAND JOB EXPERIENCE' is a newspaper headline that I have seen with my own eyes. I think you'll agree: it needed a hyphen, either between 'first' and 'hand' or between 'hand' and 'job', depending.

43

'Compound' words are simply words joined together to create a new meaning: sometimes they will come with a hyphen (mother-in-law, hand-me-down, ten-year-old); sometimes they won't (bedroom, notebook, firefly); and, in some cases, the jury's still out. Is it 'make-up' or 'makeup'? Don't ask me.

Back to hyphens and what I *can* tell you is that compound adjectives made up of a noun and an adjective (accident-prone, sports-mad, sugar-free), or a noun and a participle (computer-driven, record-breaking, thought-provoking), or an adjective and a participle (good-hearted, bad-tempered, quick-thinking), should usually be hyphenated. That said, with compound adjectives formed from the adverb 'well' and a participle (well-known, well-intentioned, well-received), or from a phrase (up-to-date, last-minute, world-famous), you should use a hyphen when the compound comes *before* the noun, but not *after*:

> Tom Cruise is a well-known good-looking actor. Having said that, he is less well known in North Korea than in South Korea, but just as good-looking.

> This is up-to-date information. At least, I have done my best to ensure that it is up to date.

And when you have a stop-off in Dubai on your flight back from India, though it's a *stop-off* you just *stop off* there — without a hyphen. The *build-up* to the trip may be considerable, but as you *build up* to it, you do so without a hyphen. The point is that a verb made up of a verb and an adverb or a preposition (like 'stop off' or 'build up') comes without a

44

hyphen when it is a verb, but has a hyphen when it is turned into a noun. But whether you were flown by an *aircrew*, an *air crew* or an *air-crew* is a matter for you to decide. Good luck.

And finally, happily, here are some of the times and places when you should use a hyphen — no question.

- Use a hyphen to separate a prefix from a name or date, e.g. 'post-Brexit', 'pre-1066'.
- Use a hyphen to stand for a common second element in all but the last word of a list, e.g. 'There are two-, three-, and four-year-olds all in the same class.'
- Use a hyphen with compound numbers from twenty-one to ninety-nine, e.g. 'thirty-one', 'fifty-five', 'seventy-two'.
- Use hyphens when writing out fractions, e.g. 'one-third', 'two-fifths', 'nine-tenths', but only when the fraction is being used as an adjective rather than a noun, e.g. 'You might guzzle one-quarter of the wine in the cask, but one quarter of your colleagues would not.'
- Use a hyphen when a number forms part of an adjectival compound, e.g. 'In the twentieth century most twentieth-century workers worked at least a forty-hour week.'

And now the dash — the punctuation mark of our times.

Dashes have been around for centuries. The word turns up in English around the year 1300 and derives from a Danish word, *daske*, meaning 'to strike' or 'to beat'. It has meant 'to move quickly' for about seven hundred years and 'to write quickly' for almost four hundred. But it's only in relatively

45

recent times that dashes have become the amazing, versatile, universally used — and, arguably, overused — punctuation marks that stand in for brackets (parentheses to Americans), commas, colons, and semi-colons.

Dashes come in two lengths:

1. The short dash, generally known as the 'en-dash'. (An *en* is a printer's unit of measurement equal to half an *em* and approximately the average width of a typeset character like the letter 'n'.)
2. The long dash, generally known as the 'em-dash'. (Yup, because an 'm' is roughly twice the width of an 'n'.)

In Britain, in the near-past, we have been using en-dashes and em-dashes indiscriminately, not realising the significant differences between them and naively assuming that one dash is as good as another. That has got to stop. The Americans are all too conscious of the differences between the en-dash and the em-dash and, in the interests of good international communication, it behoves us to come up to speed.

The en-dash is longer than a hyphen:

The em-dash is twice the length of an en-dash:

We can rattle through the en-dash pretty swiftly — it has its uses, but doesn't compare with the va-va-voom (or versatility) of the em-dash.

Essentially, the en-dash is used to represent a span or range of numbers, dates, or time. There should be no space between the en-dash and the adjacent material:

Oscar Wilde (1854–1900)

The 1894–5 season saw him at the peak of his powers.

You will discover more in chapters 12–15.

If you introduce the span or range with words such as *from* or *between*, do not use the en-dash. 'Oscar Wilde lived from 1854 to 1900' is acceptable, but 'Oscar Wilde lived from 1854–1900' is not.

What the en-dash does is pretty limited: what the em-dash can do is almost limitless. It's a gloriously versatile punctuation mark, looked down on by some old-school grammarians and snobby linguistic purists — but f—— 'em, things ain't what they used to be. The em-dash is here to stay.

Depending on the context, the em-dash can take the place of commas, colons, and brackets/parentheses and is used either solo or in a pair.

The solo em-dash is used in a variety of ways:

- To mark a pause for effect:
  I fell for her — kerpow!

- To introduce an elaboration:
  I love her — truly, madly, deeply.

- to introduce a summary:
  I love her — she is the love of my life.

- to introduce an afterthought or as a change of direction:
  I love her — but what's the point? She's a bichon cross-breed and it's against the law.

Pairs of em-dashes are used as brackets or a pair of commas might be:

- to enclose a piece of additional information:
  The moment I glimpsed her — coming down the stairs in her birthday suit — I sensed she could be the one.

- to enclose a side-thought:
  The moment I glimpsed her — how come I had forgotten Honoria already? — I knew it had to be.

- to enclose an interruption:
  The moment I glimpsed her — kerpow! — it was love at first sight.

- to enclose a comment:
  The moment I glimpsed her — men, we're all the same! — I knew it would end in ludicrous pursuit followed by humiliation.

Although em-dashes work in much the same way as commas, colons, and brackets/parentheses, they do so more obviously — with less discretion. There is a subtle difference between this:

She was lovely, and blue-eyed.

And this:

> She was lovely — and blue-eyed.

Essentially, the em-dash makes more noise than the comma — and the aside in brackets is a gentler creature (and less noticeable) than the one between em-dashes.

> She arrived from Paris (France) for Easter.

> She went on to Paris — Texas — for Christmas.

If — even having read what I have told you about commas, colons, and semi-colons — you still can't work out which ones to use when and where, em-dashes are very convenient substitutes. That said, beware of using more than two or three em-dashes in a sentence. An excess of em-dashes isn't easy on the eye, runs the risk of giving every pause the same degree of significance, and can cause confusion:

> She loved Venice — with its bridges and canals — and couldn't wait to return — preferably with Pedro — her Portuguese paramour — who had taught her so much about gondolas — and pasta — and love.

This might be a better version of that:

> She loved Venice, with its bridges and canals, and couldn't wait to return — preferably with Pedro (her Portuguese paramour) — who had taught her so much about gondolas, and pasta — and love.

Traditionally, the em-dash is used without a space to either side — but I don't like that. Most style guides — especially those in the United States — will advise you not to leave a gap either side of your em-dash. Ignore them. A gap makes what you are writing easier to read — and consequently — in my view — easier to understand.

The exception to this Brandreth Rule is when you are using your dash to indicate the missing portion of a word.

You use a double em-dash to indicate that part of a word is missing (D——— ye, sir! F——— 'em!) and you leave no gap between the letter and the dash.

If you want to imply a specific word with your dashes, you can use a series of en-dashes to show the number of letters that are missing. With 'He was an utter t———', we may not be certain whether he was a tit, a twat or a tosser. This makes it a tad clearer: 'He was a t––, a t––– and a t––––––.' (As it happens, I knew him. What a w––––––!)

Brackets (Parentheses)

What the British call 'brackets', the Americans call 'parentheses' — when they are round brackets, that is. What the Americans call 'brackets' are what the British call 'square brackets'. It doesn't cause as much confusion as the meaning of the word 'fanny' either side of the Atlantic, but it serves to underline the truth of the observation made by Oscar Wilde more than 130 years ago: 'We have really everything in common with America nowadays, except, of course, language.'

Round brackets are principally used to separate off

information that isn't essential to the meaning of the rest of the sentence. If you removed the bracketed material, the sentence would still make perfect sense — *viz*:

> It serves to underline the truth of the observation made by Oscar Wilde more than 130 years ago (in *The Canterville Ghost*): 'We have really everything in common with America nowadays, except, of course, language.'

Round brackets are also used to add additional, stand-alone material that is relevant to what has gone before but does not need to be an essential part of it.

> It serves to underline the truth of the observation made by Oscar Wilde more than 130 years ago: 'We have really everything in common with America nowadays, except, of course, language.' (The line is often incorrectly attributed to another Irish playwright, George Bernard Shaw.)

When the brackets are used to enclose a stand-alone sentence, the full stop at the end of the sentence should be placed inside the second bracket. When the brackets are used at the end of a sentence, the full stop should be placed outside, as the final punctuation:

> Oscar Wilde deserves the credit (not Bernard Shaw).

Brackets always travel in pairs and have played a pivotal role in the development of the emoji and the emoticon. As a taste of things to come, here's a pair of brackets happily helping to illustrate the meaning of the word 'fanny':

Square brackets are used principally to enclose words added by someone other than the original writer or speaker, typically in order to clarify the situation:

The author [Gyles Brandreth] was guilty of occasional lapses in both taste and judgement.

They can also be used for brackets within brackets.

Slashes

Surprisingly, the slash has been around for centuries. Over the years it has been known as the stroke, the oblique stroke, the oblique, the slant, the solidus, and the virgule — as in *virgule*, the French word for comma. This is what it looks like:

That slash is a forward slash, not to be confused with a backslash, which looks like this:

Never use a backslash in place of a slash and, unless you are a computer programmer, avoid both as much as you can. Only computer geeks properly understand the place of the backslash in the modern world. The place of the forward slash, other than in the language of computing, is limited but real.

You can use a forward slash with **poetry** when you want to record a piece of verse without setting it out as a poem. For example:

> There was a young man from Peru
> Whose limericks stopped at line two.

You could write it up like this, using the forward slash to indicate the line break:

There was a young man from Peru / Whose limericks stopped at line two.

The forward slash is also used in **fractions** (4/5ths); in writing **dates** (01/03/19); with some **abbreviations** (e.g.

c/o = care of); to indicate **time spans** (the 1914/18 war); to show **alternatives** (a win/lose situation); in place of **or** (he/she, him/her); in place of the Latin word *cum* meaning 'combined with' (a kitchen-*cum*-dining room = a kitchen/diner); in place of the Latin word *per* meaning 'through' or 'by means' (100 kilometres per hour = 100 km/h; a salary of £100 per week = a £100/week salary. [Not enough.]) (See what I did there? Threw in a pair of square brackets just to show you how they can be used. If I'm enjoying this more than you are, that's probably because I'm on drugs. Class A — I always go for top of the range. [Really?][7])

The Ellipsis

You call three dots/three full stops/three periods in a row an *ellipsis*. You call more than one of them *ellipses*. The word comes, via Latin, from the Greek for 'leaving out' — and that's precisely what an ellipsis marks: something that's been left out.

This is an ellipsis:

● ● ●

You use an ellipsis to show that something specific has been omitted:

[7] Of course not. Just joking. The only drugs I'm on are statins.

Ten, nine, eight, seven ... three, two, one — lift off!

'To be or not to be ... Whether 'tis nobler in the mind ...'

Or to suggest something unsaid, but somehow lingering in the air:

'Yes, I have known love, after a fashion ...'

In creative writing the ellipsis can be useful for introducing a change of direction:

She thought of taking her own life ... But then remembered the hen-party she was planning to go to in Magaluf.

Or for suggesting hesitation:

'My feelings are ... complicated, I suppose. That's the truth. Or perhaps, not complicated ... Confused? Er ... Yes, that's it. Confused.'

And mystery — what's coming next?

Tomorrow would be another day ...

And even for a little gentle teasing:

All we ever do is ask questions ... Why?

There has been controversy about how to place an ellipsis on the page, but I am ready to settle the issue here and now. These are the Brandreth Rules and (whatever other style guides might say) stick with these and you won't go wrong.

1. An ellipsis NEVER contains more than three dots. It's always 'Tomorrow was another day...' It's never 'Tomorrow was another day .....' — however dramatic or uncertain you want to imply the future may be. 'Three dots max' — that's the rule.

2. The three dots in the ellipsis are CONSECUTIVE. No gaps between the dots. This is correct: ... This is not: . . .

3. If the ellipsis is there as a mid-sentence hesitation, there should be no gap between the words and the ellipsis — e.g. 'My feelings are... complicated, I suppose.'

4. If the ellipsis is there to suggest a longer pause, or a thought that is trailing away, or leading somewhere new, there should be no space between the end of the first phrase and the start of the ellipsis, but a single space before the start of the new thought or sentence — e.g. 'Or perhaps, not complicated... Confused? Er... Yes, that's it. Confused.'

5. If an ellipsis is used to mark the omission of a full sentence — from a quotation, for example — put a full stop at the end of the preceding sentence, then leave a single space before placing the ellipsis and add another space before beginning the next sentence — e.g. 'Sherlock

Holmes took his bottle from the corner of the mantelpiece and his hypodermic syringe from its neat morocco case. ... Finally, he thrust the sharp point home, pressed down the tiny piston, and sank back into the velvet-lined arm-chair with a long sigh of satisfaction.'

6. If an ellipsis is used simply to indicate the omission of a number of words mid-sentence, leave a single space both before and after the ellipsis — e.g. 'I eat my pudding first and finish up with my starter ... I like to confuse my large intestine.'

The Question Mark

A question mark looks like this:

I remember the wonderful comic actor, Kenneth Williams, telling me how a London cab driver had told him that he had had the famous philosopher Bertrand Russell in the back of his cab once. Apparently, the cabbie had said to the great man: 'What's it all about, Bert?' 'What did he reply?' asked Kenneth. 'Do you know what?' said the cabbie. 'The bleeder didn't know.'

You only use a question mark after a direct question:

> What's it all about?

> What did he reply?

> Do you know what?

A question marks ends a question to which an answer is expected. It is not used with an indirect question, which is reporting a direct question and to which no answer is expected:

> The cabbie asked him if he knew what it was all about.

> Kenneth asked what the philosopher had replied.

This is a direct question, requiring a question mark:

> I am asking myself: 'What does the future hold?'

This isn't and doesn't:

> I wonder what the future holds.

Some style guides say that a question mark should never follow a rhetorical question because a rhetorical question doesn't expect or require an answer. Are they crazy? What's that about? The Brandreth Rule is that rhetorical questions do need to be followed by a question mark because, while they don't necessarily expect or require an answer, an answer is possible.

You use a question mark, too, with a statement that has a question tagged on to it:

Love conquers all, doesn't it?

At the start of 2018 the award-winning broadcaster, Jeremy Vine, launched a campaign to reduce the use of the question mark. He said on Twitter: 'I find question marks in many contexts obsolete. There is a subtler way of posing a question. Something pensive, like: "Has anyone else thought of going to live in Scotland. I have"... doesn't need a q-mark. I only use them now for a v direct enquiry: "Have you seen the car?"'

I take Jeremy's point. If he wants to ask his listeners a direct question in the hope that they would call in to his radio show or respond to his Twitter account, he would need to ask: 'Has anyone else thought of going to live in Scotland?' But if, as he suggests, he is simply musing — mulling over the idea in his head while gently planting it in yours — perhaps the question is half-way to being an indirect question and should be presented as such, without a question mark.

The use of language — and the use of punctuation — is an ever-evolving process and in this instance Jeremy may be in the vanguard of change. What do you think. [That doesn't look right, does it?] What do you think? [That's better.]

My rule-of-thumb here is: go for what looks right, feels right, sounds right in your head. 'What hope is there?' is subtly different from 'What hope is there.'

Happily, Jeremy's brother, the award-winning comedian,

Tim Vine, has no problem in using the question mark in the traditional way:

- I was in the army and the sergeant said to me: 'What does surrender mean?' I said: 'I give up!'
- This bloke said to me: 'I'm going to attack you with the neck of a guitar.' I said: 'Is that a fret?'
- I said to the gym instructor: 'Can you teach me to do the splits?' He said: 'How flexible are you?' I said: 'I can't make Tuesdays.'
- I got home, and the phone was ringing. I picked it up, and said: 'Who's speaking, please?' And a voice said: 'You are.'
- Exit signs? They're on the way out!
- Velcro? What a rip-off!

Traditionally, one question mark is all you need to serve your purpose — but that's changing, too. Jeremy Vine tells me that when texting or tweeting he will use more than one question mark if necessary. According to Jeremy, it's virtually a BBC rule now. One question mark means 'Who booked this guy?' Two question marks is a coded signal to call security.

In recent years, multiple question marks have taken on an acceptability and a significance that would have been entirely lost on Jane Austen. In the modern world of e-communication multiple question marks are used to express a heightened degree of expectation in an enquiry:

Have you caught sight of Mr Darcy????

What's Lydia up to this time????

Or, on their own, a sense of confusion:

????

Or even, despair:

??????????

The Exclamation Mark

An exclamation mark looks like this:

And you use it at the end of a word or phrase or sentence:

- to add emphasis:
  Bugger off!

- to underline emotion:
  I adore you!

- to express surprise:
  Fancy meeting you here!

- to convey, in direct speech, a shouting voice or a clear command:
  I said, 'Bugger off!'

The look of the exclamation mark goes back a thousand years (or more) and seems to derive from the Latin exclamation of joy: *io*. The word *io* was the equivalent of 'Yo!' or 'Yay!' or 'Hooray!' and medieval scribes would use it when copying out manuscripts to mark the completion of a particular passage. Gradually the '*i*' migrated above the '*o*', which eventually shrank itself into a dot like a full stop.

With the advent of printing, the exclamation of joy became known as the 'mark of admiration' and the 'sign of awe and wonder'. With the development of newspapers in the nineteenth and twentieth centuries, the exclamation mark became known by a number of nicknames: 'the screamer', 'the slammer', 'the startler', 'the gasper', 'the shriek'. In 1950s America, shorthand typists who took dictation knew it as 'the bang'. In parts of the old British Commonwealth it was known as 'the pling' — and still is. In 1960s Britain, when as a boy I acquired my first typewriter, the bang/pling/exclamation mark did not feature on the keyboard. To create it, you had to type a full stop, then backspace and type an apostrophe above it.

The reason typewriters didn't feature a key for exclamation marks is that in professional writing in the good old days you weren't expected to use them. That said, fine writers have often used them and if, like me, you are a defender of the Queen's English, you will note that royalty has always been partial to them. Queen Victoria's diaries are littered with them. Here she is in full flow in February 1840, using those marks of admiration, awe, wonder, and joy, with gay abandon:

My <u>dearest dearest dear</u> Albert sat on a footstall by my side, and his excessive love and affection gave me feelings of heavenly love and happiness, I never could have <u>hoped</u> to have felt before! He clasped me in his arms, and we kissed each other again and again! His beauty, his sweetness and gentleness, — really how can I ever be thankful enough to have such a <u>Husband</u>! ... to lie by his side, and in his arms, and on his dear bosom, and be called by names of tenderness, I have never yet heard used to me before — was bliss beyond belief!

When day dawned (for we did not sleep much) and I beheld that beautiful face by my side, it was more than I can express! Oh! was ever woman so blessed as I am.

This, of course, was her wedding night, so, not surprisingly, her account of it featured a right royal double-bang: 'I <u>never never</u> spent such an evening!!'

F. Scott Fitzgerald would not have been amused. 'Cut out all these exclamation points,' he said. 'An exclamation point is like laughing at your own joke.'

Of course, moderation in all things is a good rule in life, but a well-placed exclamation mark does serve a distinct purpose — and more than one is acceptable these days when circumstances demand.

'What the fuck???!!!'

In 1962, an American advertising man, Martin K. Speckter, came up with the notion of a new punctuation mark that could express both excitement and surprise.

He toyed with calling the new mark an 'exclamoquest' or an 'exclarotive', but eventually settled on an 'inter-robang' — from the Latin *interrogatio* and the American *bang*. This is what it looks like:

The mark was quite widely used in the 1960s and then fell out of favour. What was that about‽

These days 'what's that about?!' is most simply expressed with a question mark followed by an exclamation mark. An exclamation mark inside parentheses is used to suggest sarcasm:

> I hated being his secretary. Whenever he was dictating a letter, half-way through he'd say, 'How about a bang at this juncture?' Very amusing(!)

The exclamation mark is not a subtle piece of punctuation, but it is expressive.

- ! on its own can mean 'Wow!'
- !! can mean 'Wow! Wow!'
- !!! can mean 'Yes!'
- !!!! means 'Oh my God!'
- !!!!! means 'Aaaaargh!'

Quotation Marks

'I always have a quotation for everything,' said Dorothy L. Sayers. 'It saves original thinking.'

I love quotations. 'A quotation in a speech, article or book is like a rifle in the hands of an infantryman,' said the Irish playwright Brendan Behan; 'it speaks with authority.' Exactly. 'An apt quotation is like a lamp which flings its light over the whole sentence,' said Letitia Elizabeth Landon. I couldn't have put it better myself. That's the point: that's why I'm quoting her. And I don't feel embarrassed about how often I resort to quotation. After all, as Oscar Wilde pointed out: 'Most people are other people. Their thoughts are someone else's opinions, their lives a mimicry, their passions a quotation.'

I have a passion for quotations. I am the editor of the *Oxford Dictionary of Humorous Quotations*. My wife is the compiler of a dictionary of theatrical quotations. We rarely attempt to say anything original to each other. We simply exchange other people's brilliant banter. (At breakfast this morning, she offered me this gem from P. G. Wodehouse: 'He had just about enough intelligence to open his mouth when he wanted to eat, but certainly no more.' I didn't rise to the bait. I responded with another Wodehouse line that I knew she'd be happy to endorse: 'At the age of eleven or thereabouts women acquire a poise and an ability to handle difficult situations which a man, if he is lucky, manages to achieve somewhere in the later seventies.')

Of course, it is quotations I love. You won't find me

messing about in 'quotes'. (Nor 'invites', come to that.) To me and most of my generation, 'quote' (and 'invite') are verbs, not nouns. What you quote is a quotation: it isn't a quote — in my book. And, later in my book, I will explain why and you can decide on which side of the fence you want to land.

Meanwhile, let's get to grips with quotation marks, known as 'quotes' to some, I acknowledge, and as 'inverted commas' or 'speech marks' to many. They come in pairs and they look like this:

‘ ’

Or this:

“ ”

Quotation marks are used to mark the beginning and end of direct speech — *viz*:

'You don't need a bigger screen,' she said.
'Really?' he replied.
'Yes,' she went on. 'Just move the sofa closer to
the one you've got.'

66

In British English, single inverted commas are used more frequently than double ones. In American English it's the other way around. Either is acceptable, but having made your choice, stick with it. You only use both sorts if you happen to have a quote within a quote — or, as I think of it, a quotation within a quotation:

> She said, 'Do you think "To be or not to be"
> is the most famous quotation in the English language?'

In American English, any punctuation associated with the word or phrase within the quotation mark should come before the closing quotation mark:

> Money talks. All mine ever seems to say is 'Goodbye.'

In British English, the associated punctuation is placed outside the closing quotation mark:

> Money talks. All mine ever seems to say is 'Goodbye'.

In British and American English, if your quotation lasts longer than a paragraph, you put a quotation mark at the start of the opening paragraph and at the beginning of each subsequent paragraph, but no quotation marks at the end of each paragraph until you reach the end of the whole quotation and the closing quotation mark goes there.

Quotation marks can be used, too, to enclose the titles of books, movies, plays, etc., foreign words and phrases, and slang expressions:

'Hamlet' by William Shakespeare is reckoned by many to be his 'chef d'œuvre' — his 'pièce de résistance'. It's certainly the 'bomb.com' as far as I'm concerned.

Equally acceptable (and preferred by some) is the use of italics in place of quotation marks:

> *Hamlet* by William Shakespeare is reckoned by many to be his *chef d'oeuvre* — his *pièce de résistance*. It's certainly the *bomb.com* as far as I'm concerned.

Quotation marks, not italics, are what's required when you are using a word or phrase and want to give it a sarcastic or ironic edge — *viz*:

> She's 'curvy'. [She's fat.]

> He's a 'cool dude'. [He's anything but.]

As well as for indicating titles — e.g. 'Just a minute, I'll check what time *Just a Minute* is going to be on' — and foreign phrases — e.g. 'Does *in loco parentis* mean "my dad's an engine driver"?' — italics — *a cursive, sloping script like this* — are used to add emphasis — e.g.:

> In my house *I'm* the boss. My wife is merely the decision-maker.

In handwritten English, you can underline what in print you might have put in italics. <u>Underlining in print</u>

does not look attractive. In print, if you want emphasis, you have *italic* and **bold** at your disposal.

The Asterisk

The asterisk is the little star symbol that you find above the '8' key on your keyboard. The word comes, via Latin, from a Greek word meaning 'little star'. In 'younger and happier days',[8] when the world knew more decorum, asterisks were used to show the omission of one or more letters in words like sh*t or f*** or b******s, or in names to help disguise them — e.g. 'President T**** is a w****r.'[9] Asterisks can still be used for that purpose, but their principal role these days is as a symbol to refer readers to a note at the foot of the page.

Hip American writers also drop them in (in pairs) as alternatives to brackets — or em-dashes — to indicate an aside serving as a comment on what is being said * raises eyebrow * if you get my drift.

---

[8] It's a favourite phrase of mine, borrowed from Miss Prism, the governess in Oscar Wilde's play *The Importance of Being Earnest*. I only threw it in to have an excuse for a footnote. Thank you for joining me down here. While we're here, do you have a favourite Wilde quotation? Mine used to be, 'Be yourself; everyone else is already taken' — until I discovered that there is no evidence he ever said it.
[9] President Truman was indeed a wonder. Harry S. Truman, the thirty-third President of the United States, was unique: the only president to have a middle initial but no name to go with it.

3. Apostrophe Now

Here are words that I have seen with my own eyes — on ten separate signs and one gravestone. Read, reader, and despair.

Tattoo's

Open Sunday's

No Dogs Were Afraid

Teacher's Break Room

Ladies and Mens Outfitters

St Lukes Hospital Main Entrance

Hard Hat's required beyond this point

Karen's Bit's & Bob's at Bargain Price's

The Birmingham Childrens Hospital NHS Trust

One of the best of mother's — may she rest in peace

Dentists look after your teeth. Who looks after theirs'? Colgate!

It's a pyramid of shame, isn't it? I am confident that you feel it is because, according to every public opinion survey on the subject I've seen, the misplaced apostrophe — and the missing apostrophe — are the two linguistic horrors that distress most of us the most. Look around as you walk down any street and they hit you in the face like a series of Smokin' Joe Frazier's left hooks. They're unbearable — and everywhere.

Incredibly, not everyone feels the same way. I once met Dr John Wells, Emeritus Professor of Phonetics at University College, London, who maintains the apostrophe is 'a waste of time'. George Bernard Shaw (a fellow vegetarian and, in so many ways, a great man[10]) described apostrophes as 'uncouth bacilli'. Intellectuals on both sides of the Atlantic have campaigned for the abolition of the apostrophe over the years, on the grounds that in spoken English it is irrelevant, and in written English it's largely unnecessary and causes more trouble than it's worth.

I beg to differ. As Mr Russell, the head of English at the Park School, Baltimore (where I taught during my gap year in the 1960s), used to say: 'Without the apostrophe, how are you going to tell the difference between feeling your nuts and feeling you're nuts?' I believe in the place, power, and value of the apostrophe.

Once upon a time, in the United States, the war against the apostrophe was led by a remarkable man of letters called Steven Byington (1869–1957). He was a noted linguist (fluent in twelve languages) who translated the Bible and was kind to animals, but he had a bee in his bonnet when it came to the apostrophe and believed passionately that 'the language would be none the worse for its abolition'. That Byington (who was undeniably brilliant) felt as he did

[10] When asked, 'If there was a fire at the National Gallery, which painting would you save?' he replied, 'The one nearest the door.'

puzzled me until I discovered his secret: he was an anarchist. That explained everything.

Give up on the apostrophe and you're giving in to chaos. Without the apostrophe, there's linguistic anarchy. The apostrophe is the symbol of our cause — the mark we need emblazoned on our banners. If we go weak or wobbly in our defence of the apostrophe, we are on the slippery slope to incomprehensibility and confusion.

The late, great English novelist, Kingsley Amis, liked to illustrate the importance of the role of the apostrophe by quoting one seven-word sentence in which the placing or the absence of an apostrophe would transform the meaning of the words:

- Those things over there are my husband's. (Meaning: Those things over there belong to my husband.)
- Those things over there are my husbands'. (Meaning: Those things over there belong to my husbands — I have more than one.)
- Those things over there are my husbands. (Meaning: I'm married to those men over there.)

Another considerable man of letters is my friend Bernard C. Lamb, Emeritus Reader in Genetics at Imperial College, London, and President of the Queen's English Society. He likes to illustrate the power of the apostrophe with the example of the headline: BRITON'S BATTLE FATIGUE. This was an account of one Briton's battle fatigue. Had the apostrophe followed the 's' it would have indicated the battle fatigue of more than one Briton. Without the apostrophe — in Bernard Shaw's and Steven Byington's dark, anarchic world — the headline changes its meaning altogether, BATTLE transmogrifying from a noun to a verb and the headline — BRITONS BATTLE FATIGUE — suggesting a nation united in a struggle against exhaustion.

Okay, you get the message. Without apostrophes: Armageddon. We need 'em. And we need to know how to use 'em. Read on.

This is what an apostrophe looks like:

> ,

And it is used to do one of two things:

1. It is there to show **possession** — to indicate that a thing or a person belongs or relates to someone or something. (*Possession* is a novel by A. S. Byatt: yes, *Possession* is A. S. Byatt's novel.)
2. It is there to show **omission** — to indicate that letters are missing. (It is her best-known novel: yes, it's her best-known one.)

Possession – The Rules

- with singular nouns and most personal names, simply add an apostrophe followed by the letter s:

Yesterday's news
The gamekeeper's mistress
Lady Chatterley's lover

73

- with personal names that end in -s, add an apostrophe followed by a further s when you would normally pronounce an extra s if you said the word out loud:

This is Gyles's book
Those are Dickens's novels
Camilla is Charles's wife
That is Martin Rees's telescope

Annoyingly, there are occasional exceptions to this rule, notably in relation to the names of organisations, companies, and brands. Writing about the miracles of St Thomas you would be correct to refer to 'St Thomas's miracles', but when it comes to the London hospital it is known as 'St Thomas' Hospital'. You might want to refer to 'Starbucks's' range of sandwiches — because that's how you say it — but Starbucks want you to think of them simply as 'Starbucks' so they eschew the apostrophe altogether. It's 'Starbucks Coffee' — and that's that.

- with personal names that end in -s but when said out loud are not spoken with an extra s, you just add an apostrophe after the -s:

Starbucks' argument did not impress
the Inland Revenue
Mellors' performance much impressed
Lady Chatterley

- with a plural noun that already ends in -s, you simply add an apostrophe after the s:

> The new term at the boys' school
> begins in two weeks' time
> The horses' stable doors have been bolted

- with a plural noun that doesn't end in -s, you add an apostrophe plus an s:

> Yet again the women's team
> scored better than the men's team

- apart from Starbucks, the only time when you do not need to use an apostrophe at all to show possession is with the group of words known as *possessive pronouns*. Here they are:

> his
> hers
> ours
> yours
> theirs

And they mean *belonging to him, her, us, you,* or *them.* The same goes for the so-called *possessive determiners*:

> his
> her

its

our

your

their

meaning *belonging to* or *associated with him, her, it, us, you,* or *them.*

Given we are celebrating the Queen's English here, note that while there is no apostrophe in *his, hers, ours, yours,* and *theirs,* there is one in *one's.*

And be sure never to get *its* (the possessive pronoun) confused with *it's* (meaning *it is*). Remember:

- *Its* is possessive, so all the letters hug to one another.
  - *It's* means *it is,* so if in doubt spell it out.

      'This is the age of Twitter. Its time has come.' That makes sense.
      'This is the age of Twitter. It is time has come.' That doesn't.
      Its easy — wrong! It is easy, so it's easy — right?

Omission — The Rules

An apostrophe is used to show when letters (or numbers) have been omitted:

      It's obvious,
      isn't it?

76

Well, it's obvious with *it's* because the '*i*' is missing from *is*. It's slightly less obvious with *isn't* because you are combining two words as well as dropping the '*o*' from *is not*.

- **I'm** is short for **I am**.
- **You're** is short for **you are**.
- **He'll** is short for **he will**.
- **She'd** is short for **she had** or **she would**.
- **Wouldn't** is short for **would not**.
- **Shan't** is short for **shall not** (and in some old books you might find it written as **sha'n't**).
- Fish **'n'** chips is short for fish **and** chips.
- The **fo'c'sle** — also known as the **fo'c's'le** — is short for the **forecastle**, the upper deck of a sailing ship forward of the foremast.[11]
- We think of the roaring **'20s** as the roaring **'twenties** — and that's the decade, the **1920s** or **nineteen-twenties**, when our grandparents were having a gay old time enjoying their roaring twenties. [See what I did there? — illustrating the difference the presence or absence of an apostrophe makes.]

Agreed: it's all a bit of a **pick 'n' mix**, especially when you remember that words like influenza and telephone were

---

[11] Where you might find the **boatswain**, or **bo's'n**, **bos'n**, or **bosun**: the petty officer or crew member in charge of a ship's deck and hull. The omission of sounds or letters from within a word — as in **fo'c'sle** or **bosun** for **forecastle** and **boatswain** — is called 'syncope', pronounced 'sincopee'. It's how we come to pronounce these splendid English names as 'Chumli', 'Fanshaw', 'Marchbanks', and 'Roxley', and when they are written as **Cholmondeley**, **Featherstonehaugh**, **Marjoribanks**, and **Wriothesley**.

once abbreviated to **'flu** and **'phone**, but now have lost their apostrophes. Because I'm quite old-school I still call a violoncello a **'cello**.

Apostrophes and Plurals

The rule is that you should **NOT** use an apostrophe to form the plurals of:

nouns,
names,
abbreviations,
or dates made up of numbers

Instead you just add an -s — or an -es if the noun in question forms its plural with -es:

apple / apples
banana / bananas
cat / cats
class / classes
iris / irises
lens / lenses
dollar / dollars
Euro / euros
MP / MPs
Daisy [the name] / Daisys
daisy [the flower] / daisies
1920 / 1920s
apostrophe / apostrophes

We shall be exploring controversial plurals in a few pages' time. The point here and now is whether or not the plural of *referendum* is **referendums** or **referenda**; it is never **referendum's**.

With the plural of a family name, you just add an -s. It's the Brandreths, the Kardashians, and the Trumps you need to keep up with, never the Brandreth's, the Kardashian's, or the Trump's. When the family name ends with -s, -x, -z, -ch, or -sh, you do **NOT** add an apostrophe: you add *-es*, keeping up with the Joneses, the Fairfaxes, the Rodriguezes, the Norwiches, and the Bushes.

The tiny exception to this 'no apostrophes with plurals' rule comes in the case of single letters and single numbers if adding an apostrophe aids clarity. 'I've dotted the is and crossed the ts' looks wrong and reads confusingly, so 'I've dotted the i's and crossed the t's' is allowed. The same goes for 'Mind your p's and q's', but only because 'ps' could be misinterpreted as an abbreviation of 'postscript'.

I don't think you need an apostrophe here: 'How many 5s are there in the number 5,555?' But some authorities say you do. There are times when the language is undoubtedly at 6s and 7s ... or is that 6's and 7's ... or sixes and sevens? No one can quite agree. The general feeling among the authorities I've consulted seems to be that, online and in emails, numbers should be written using digits, but when writing for the record you should definitely use words for numbers for one through to nine, probably use words for numbers for ten to twenty, and possibly use words for numbers to get from twenty-one to one hundred. In formal writing, when only two words are

involved, the preference is for words rather than digits —
so it's one hundred, but 123, three thousand, but 3,333.

That said, remember that an apostrophe should **NEVER**
be used to form the plural of ordinary nouns, names, abbreviations, or numbers or dates. Take another look at the
pyramid of shame and shudder:

Tattoo's
No! It's 'Tattoos'

Open Sunday's
No! It's 'Open Sundays'

No Dogs Were Afraid
No! It's 'No Dogs We're Afraid'

Teacher's Break Room
No! It's 'Teachers' Break Room'
(Unless, of course, it's one of those lovely little village
schools where there is only one teacher.)

Ladies and Mens Outfitters
No! It's 'Ladies' and Men's Outfitters'
(Though, intriguingly, when two owners of the same
thing are named in the same sentence, the apostrophe
comes only after the second name, not after both; so if
the owners of the Ladies' and Gents' Outfitters in
question are called Jack and Jill, it would be 'Jack and
Jill's Outfitters'. Nobody said this was going to be easy.
[If you happen to be Japanese, well done getting this
far — but I'd junk the book now if I were you. I gave

up on your language at Lesson 3 and everyone says
Japanese is a doddle compared with English.
(Yes, it is *compared with*. We will get to the matter
of *compared to* in due course.)]

St Lukes Hospital Main Entrance
No! It's 'St Luke's Hospital Main Entrance'

Hard Hat's required beyond this point
No! It's 'Hard Hats required beyond this point'

Karen's Bit's & Bob's at Bargain Price's
No! It's 'Karen's Bits & Bobs at Bargain Prices'

The Birmingham Childrens Hospital NHS Trust
No! It's 'The Birmingham Children's
Hospital NHS Trust'

One of the best of mother's — may she rest in peace
No! It's 'One of the best of mothers — may
she rest in peace'
(Unless they've buried her with one of her famous fruit
cakes, possibly illustrated on the gravestone, in which
case it could well be 'one of the best of mother's' . . .
Either way, may she rest in peace.[12])

Dentists look after your teeth. Who looks
after theirs'? Colgate!

[12] I once came across a small gravestone that carried the name and
dates of the deceased, followed by the inscription: 'Let her RIP'.

No! It's 'Dentists look after your teeth. Who looks after theirs? Colgate!'

The misplaced apostrophe is sometimes called the 'grocer's apostrophe' because of the frequency with which it is allegedly seen on signs in grocers' shops advertising 'Potato's', 'Tomato's', and 'Runner bean's'. To me, quite as annoying as the misplaced apostrophe is the missing apostrophe. At the 2018 Oscars' ceremony in Los Angeles, Emma Watson, the British actress, star of the *Harry Potter* films, and English Literature graduate of Brown University, wanted to signal her support for the post-Weinstein #MeToo Time's Up campaign to end sexual harassment in the movie industry. She chose to do so by sporting a sizeable tattoo on the inside of her left arm. Unfortunately it read 'Times Up' — without an apostrophe.

4. Spelling Is Big Potatoes

Do you remember the time the American Vice-President, Dan Quayle, misspelled the word 'potato'? It was in 1992. Quayle was visiting Luis Muñoz Rivera Elementary School in Trenton, New Jersey, and decided to join in a classroom spelling bee. Twelve-year-old William Figueroa had just written 'potato' on the board. The Vice-President stepped up to correct him, taking the stick of chalk from the child and confidently adding an 'e' to the end of the word to create 'potatoe'. Quayle later confessed in his memoirs, *Standing Firm*: 'It was more than a gaffe. It was a "defining moment" of the worst imaginable kind. I can't overstate how discouraging and exasperating the whole event was.'

Like it or not, these days your spelling defines you. It was not always so. William Shakespeare — without doubt the greatest writer who ever wrote — lived and worked before the age of consistent spelling, or punctuation. He spelled (or is that *spelt*?) his own name at least half a dozen different ways. When the First Folio, the first near-complete collection of his plays, was published in 1623, it was described on the title page as being:

Mr. WILLIAM
SHAKESPEARES
COMEDIES,

HISTORIES, &
TRAGEDIES
Published according to the True Originall Copies

Note the missing apostrophe after Shakespeare and the original spelling of 'originall'.

In his day Shakespeare was known as everything from 'Shaxper' to 'Shakespeare'. By the eighteenth century he was known generally as 'Shakespear'. From the late eighteenth through the early nineteenth century, 'Shakspeare' was the preferred variation. In the Victorian era the spelling 'Shakspere' was used in the belief that it was 'authentic' because that is how, at least on a few occasions, Shakespeare was believed to have signed his name himself.

Until the eighteenth century there was no standardised (or is that standardized?) English spelling. That began to change in the aftermath of the publication, on 15 April 1755, of *A Dictionary of the English Language* by the great Dr Samuel Johnson, polymath, poet, biographer, and wit. (He was the fellow who described second marriage as 'the triumph of hope over experience' and declared that 'when a man is tired of London, he is tired of life'.) There were English dictionaries before Johnson's, of course, but their quality was variable, which was why, in the summer of 1746, a group of London booksellers got together and offered Johnson a fee of 1,500 guineas (around a quarter of a million pounds in today's money) to produce an authoritative new dictionary as 'a faithful record of the language people used'. Dr Johnson (also famous for saying 'Nothing ... will ever be attempted, if all possible objections must be first overcome') thought he'd give it a go and promised to do the job within three years. In the event, he managed it in seven, coming up with 42,773 dictionary entries, including such gems as these:

- Lexicographer: A writer of dictionaries; a harmless drudge, that busies himself in tracing the original, and detailing the signification of words.
- Monsieur: A term of reproach for a Frenchman.
- Oats: A grain, which in England is generally given to horses, but in Scotland supports the people.

On the whole, Johnson offered sound definitions and provided spellings for words that came to be regarded as 'correct'. Indeed, until the arrival of the *Oxford English Dictionary* at the end of the nineteenth century, Johnson's was regarded as the pre-eminent English dictionary – outside of America. In the USA, in 1828, Noah Webster — sometime lawyer, teacher, essayist, abolitionist, and father of eight — produced a rival work: *An American Dictionary of the English Language*. Webster did not approve of Dr Johnson's idiosyncrasy, nor of his lifestyle. He maintained that Johnson had 'prepared his manuscripts in haste' because he was 'naturally indolent and seldom wrote until he was urged by want'. Webster was more diligent than Johnson, no doubt; more fastidious, too; and much more interested in spelling. Webster wanted to reform English spelling altogether and make words look as they sounded. His suggested improvements to English spelling included:

Ake *for* ache
Cloke *for* cloak

Dawter *for* daughter
Greef *for* grief
Grotesk *for* grotesque
Iland *for* island
Masheen *for* machine
Porpess *for* porpoise
Soop *for* soup
Steddy *for* steady
Wimmin *for* women

You can see what he was trying to do and it does make sense, but apart from 'wimmin' none of the above has gained much traction.[13]

Where Webster did succeed, however, was in persuading his fellow Americans to drop the silent 'u' from words like 'color', 'endeavor', 'flavor', and 'humor'; to turn 'centre' into 'center' and 'theatre' into 'theater'; to make 'defence' 'defense', 'draught' 'draft', 'gaol' 'jail', and 'plough' 'plow'. He was a proselytising spelling obsessive who pioneered and promoted the competitive spelling bee. With his two bestsellers, *The American Spelling Book* (1783) and *The Elementary Spelling Book* (1829), he established American-English spelling as we know it. Or don't know it, as the case may be.

Noah Webster died in 1843. A hundred and seventy-five years later I have been dipping in to the Twitter-talk of contemporary young Americans, most of whom might

---

[13] Without knowing that Webster had come up with it first, some feminists in the twentieth century adopted 'wimmin' as an alternative to 'women' simply because it did not contain the word 'men' within it.

not do too well in a strictly judged spelling bee but many of whom appear to have taken to heart Webster's notion of writing words as they sound. This is Generation Z in full flood, courtesy of The Poke:[14]

- Have the courage to speak to me face to face, no fighting. Let's be adults and talk it out. Or barry the hatchet. #Itneverbotheredmeanyway.
- I live bicuriously through your tweets.
- i smell like mens colon
- You can take your monday through friday business hours and ram them up your dairy air, young lady.
- Sometimes i snap at ppl on twitter bcuz im insecure. Its a defense magnesium
- I think my gramma got die of beaties
- I have no clue why people don't like hammy downs. I'll gladly take everyone's! Who doesn't like free clothes?
- I can't date a girl who is lack toe tolerance. We couldn't even go out for ice cream!
- Goodnight, Yall mindgrain headache is coming back!
- I love having sex with my boyfriend but he never makes me organism
- i would imagine jay z said something out of hand but we all know how women overyact

[14] The Poke is an online newsfeed. Generation Z (also known as Gen Z, iGeneration, iGen, and Post-Millennials) are people born since around the year 2000 who have been familiar with social media and the iCulture all their lives.

- The cream sickle jacket with the brown quarter roy pants now that's a blood bath!
- Mom said she was running some aarons at the store, but I need her here to help me with HW because I think I have 8oHD
- the seizure salad from mcdonalds is so good
- my friend looks like miley
  here comes the low selfstream
- I rather b skinny den have sellulight I tell u dat much #justsayin
- To all the Troops in the Army, The Navy and The Veterans, Thank you for protecting and severing our country! @WWE #Troops @TributeToTroops
- Michael strayhand trying to speak on national television like he don't have a speech peppermint.
- I'm committing sue aside and Justin in all white is the cause of it
- God gave you a second chance, never take anything for granite

As The Poke says, 'Sumtimes people tweet and there spelling isn't quite what it should bee.' But does it matter? The spelling's adrift, the punctuation random, and capital letters conspicuous by their absence, but we got the message, didn't we?

If punctuation and consistent spelling didn't trouble Shakespeare, why should they bother us? In a nutshell, because we aren't Shakespeare and, like it or not, we live in a world that judges by appearances. When Dan Quayle misspelled potato, the whole world mocked: 'He can't even spell potato! What else can't he do?'

Of course, the poor man already had form. The Veep's special way with the English language was something to savour/savor — *viz* these choice Quaylisms:

- We understand the importance of having the bondage between the parent and the child.
- What a waste it is to lose one's mind, or not to have a mind is being very wasteful, how true that is.
- I believe we are on an irreversible trend towards more freedom and democracy, but that could change.
- One word sums up probably the responsibility of any vice-president, and that one word is 'to be prepared'.
- I believe that I've made good judgments in the past, and I think I've made good judgments in the future.
- The future will be better tomorrow.
- I made a misstatement and I stand by all my misstatements.
- I was recently on a tour of Latin America, and the only regret I have was that I didn't study Latin harder in school so I could converse with those people.

Actually, he never said the last one. The first seven were the genuine article — pure, unadulterated Quayle — but the last (and best) was invented by a satirically minded humorist, 'put out there', and widely believed to have been actually uttered by the Vice-President. Look it up online and you will find it attributed to Quayle. That's what happens when you can't spell 'potato'.

Yes, if you can't spell, people may think you're ignorant, ill-educated, or stupid. That may be unfair. If you suffer from dyslexia, it's certainly unjust.[15] But it's an unfair, unjust world at times, and all the research suggests that the better your spelling is, the higher your income will be. The more effectively you can communicate the more successful you will be in every area of your life. Good spelling is part of good communication. But no one said it was easy.

When my father was a boy, he learned[16] this poem by heart. It was one of his favourites, because he loved word-play, and it illustrates brilliantly the peculiar challenges of English spelling.

> I take it you already know
> Of tough and bough and cough and dough?
> Others may stumble, but not you,
> On hiccough, thorough, lough and through?
> Well done! And now you wish, perhaps,
> To learn of less familiar traps?
>
> Beware of heard, a dreadful word
> That looks like beard and sounds like bird,

[15] Dyslexic 'jokes' are now properly taboo. My mother was a remedial teacher who specialised in helping children with dyslexia. I used to say that she was the founder of the charity 'Mothers Against Dyslexia' (known by the acronym DAM) — until she stopped me.
[16] 'Learned' is as acceptable as 'learnt' and in the US more so.

And dead: it's said like bed, not bead —
For goodness sake don't call it 'deed'!
Watch out for meat and great and threat
(They rhyme with suite and straight and debt).

A moth is not a moth in mother,
Nor both in bother, broth in brother,
And here is not a match for there,
Nor dear and fear for bear and pear,
And then there's dose and rose and lose —
Just look them up — and goose and choose,
And cork and work and card and ward,
And font and front and word and sword,
And do and go and thwart and cart —
Come, come, I've hardly made a start!
A dreadful language? Man alive,
I'd mastered it when I was five!

Indeed, learning the language — and the spelling that goes with it — from early childhood is the secret of success. The sooner you start, the better. (If ever you meet a French person who speaks perfect English with an accurate English accent, it will be because they learned the language before the age of seven. After that, their vocabulary may be superb, but they will sound like Gérard Depardieu or Vanessa Paradis.)

Mastering spelling is not easy, but it is essential. As the hapless Dan Quayle is supposed to have said (but didn't): 'If we do not succeed, then we run the risk of failure.' We've got to try.

Fortunately, there are rules.

Unfortunately, they are not that helpful.

Spelling Rules

1. 'I' before 'E' Except after 'C'

This is the most famous of all the spelling rules — and the most frustrating. For a start, people get the rule all wrong.

It's 'i' before 'e' except after 'c' — except
when your foreign neighbour Keith receives
eight counterfeit beige sleighs
from feisty caffeinated weightlifters!

The point is: the rule is not 'i' before 'e' except after 'c'. The rule is:

It's 'i' before 'e' except after 'c'
if the vowel sound rhymes with 'bee'

That mostly works — e.g.:

achieve
believe
brief
chief
deceive
fiend
receipt
receive

But it doesn't always — e.g.:

caffeine
plebeian
protein
seize
species

And nowadays, when regional accents are held in the highest regard, it's not always possible to agree on what does or doesn't rhyme with 'bee'. How do you pronounce 'forfeit', 'counterfeit', 'surfeit'? Is it with a long 'ee' as in 'bee' or a short one as in 'bit'? And is your 'sheikh' as in 'chic' (which does rhyme with 'bee') or as in 'shake' (which doesn't)? Some say 'heinous' as in 'penis', others say 'heinous' as in 'anus'. Is it 'neither' pronounced 'neether' and is 'either' 'eether'? Exactly. Let's call the whole thing off.

This rule is fraught with pitfalls and exceptions. Yes, most words where the vowel sound doesn't rhyme with 'bee' are spelled with an 'ei' — e.g.:

deign
eider
feint
heir
reign
vein
weigh

But if you try to rely on the rule, you will find it a false friend. Yup, 'friend' is a fiend when it comes to the spelling rulebook. It does not rhyme with 'bee', but it requires an 'ie'. Weird or what?

2. 'C' or 'S' — Which Should It Be?

When it comes to the practice where the doctors practise, the words 'practice' and 'practise' sound the same, so how can you tell which should have the 'c' and which the 's'?

Here the rule for British English is that **the noun has a 'c' and the verb has an 's'** — and to help you remember the rule there's a neat mnemonic:

I advise you not to give advice

The mnemonic is useful because with the verb 'advise' (rhyming with 'eyes') and the noun 'advice' (rhyming with 'nice') you can *hear* the difference between the words. Use this device I've devised and I prophesy: you won't confuse your 's' with your 'c' in future — until you get to America. There my prophecy could come a cropper; because in the United States, when it comes to the 'c'/'s' question, their answers vary.

For 'advice' and 'advise', and 'device' and 'devise', American English goes along with the British way and the 'c' is used in the noun and the 's' with the verb. On the other hand, in the United States, 'practice' is considered perfect. It is spelled 'practice' both as a verb and as a noun. In the US, 'practise' is not used at all. In Canada, 'practise' is still used as a verb, but less frequently with every passing year.

American English uses 'license' for both the noun and the verb. In America, the British 'defence', 'offence', and 'pretence' become 'defense', 'offense', and 'pretense'; but the derivatives 'defensive', 'offensive', and 'pretension' come with an 's' on both sides of the Atlantic. 'Pretentious', of course, is spelled with neither an 's' nor a 'c', but with a 't'.

Some people believe that it was while studying the niceties of British and American spelling that the Norwegian artist Edvard Munch painted his masterpiece, 'The Scream'.

3. The Prefix Rule

How come 'misspell' has two 's's when 'disappear' only has one? With a word that starts with a prefix, the rule is: **both the prefix and the word remain unchanged.** So you combine 'mis-' with 'spell' and 'dis-' with 'appear' — it's as simple as that. That's why 'interrelated' has a double 'r', but 'interact' only has the one. Separate the prefix from the word and you shouldn't go far wrong.

PREFIX	MEANING	EXAMPLES
anti-	against	antifreeze
ante-	before	antenatal
de-	opposite	defrost
dis-	not, opposite of	disappear
en-, em-	cause to	encode, embody
fore-	before	forecast
il-	not	illiterate

in-, im-	not	injustice, impossible
inter-	between	interact
mid-	middle	midway
mis-	wrongly	misspell
non-	not	nonsense
over-	over	overlook
pre-	before	prefix
re-	again	return
semi-	half	semicircle
sub-	under	submarine
super-	above	superstar
trans-	across	transgender
un-	not	unfriendly
under-	under	underwater

What the L?

But when you get two words combining, it's different. We combine 'well' and 'come' and get 'welcome'; we combine 'all' and 'together' and get 'altogether'. Watch out when there's an 'l' about.

4. The Suffix Rules

A suffix is a letter or a group of letters added to the end of a word — *viz*:

SUFFIX	MEANING	EXAMPLES
-able, -ible	capable of	comfortable, incredible
-al, -ial	having the characteristics of	personal, convivial

-ed	past-tense verbs	laughed, loved
-en	made of	wooden, silken
-er	comparative	bigger, better
-er, -or	one who	worker, actor
-est	superlative	biggest, best
-ful	full or full of	handful, careful
-ic	having characteristics of	linguistic, sarcastic
-ing	verb form	dancing, prancing
-ion, -tion, -ation, -ition	act or process	opinion, revolution, domination, partition
-ity, -ty	state of	humility, infinity
-ive, -ative, -itive	adjective form of a noun	expensive, palliative, competitive
-less	without	topless, fearless
-ly	adverb ending	precisely, quickly
-ment	action or process	enjoyment, embarrassment
-ness	state of, condition of	awareness, tiredness
-ous, -eous, -ious	possessing the qualities of	generous, hideous, anxious
-s, -es	plural	girls, boxes
-y	acting as specified	happy, lazy

And now for the suffix spelling rules:

Consonant Suffixes
Where the suffix begins with a consonant, the main word does not normally change — e.g. *normal* + *ly* gives you *normally*; *hand* + *ful* gives you *handful*; *top* + *less* gives you *topless*; *precise* + *ly* gives you *precisely*.

E — But You've Got to Be Careful

When an 'e' comes at the end of the main word, take care. That 'e' is sometimes dropped — e.g. *true* + *ly* becomes *truly* and *due* + *ly* becomes *duly*; but *care* + *less* becomes *careless*, not *carless*, which means something different altogether. This is a rule you can dispense with if it's likely to cause confusion: you follow the rule for *die* and *dying*, but you don't for *dye* and *dyeing*. Yes, it is a tad confusing — especially when I tell you that both *likable* and *likeable* are acceptable spellings.

Vowel Suffixes

Where the suffix begins with a vowel, if the main word ends with an 'e', the rule is: you drop the 'e' — e.g. 'love'/'loving', 'dominate'/'domination'. But — stay focussed, please — that 'e' remains if the letter before it is a 'c' or a 'g', so that the word with the suffix *sounds* like the main word sounded before the suffix was added. To turn 'date' into 'datable' is easy: you just drop the 'e'. To turn 'peace' into 'peaceable' or 'outrage' into 'outrageous', you don't drop the 'e'. If you did, you run the risk of pronouncing the words incorrectly, with a hard 'c' or 'g' — e.g. 'peaKable', 'outraGHous'. That said, there are exceptions to this rule, too. Both 'aging' and 'ageing' are acceptable.

Y Not

When adding a suffix to a word that ends in a 'y' but is preceded by a consonant — e.g. 'happy', 'stuffy', 'silly' — the 'y' is replaced by an 'i' — giving you 'happier', 'stuffiness', 'silliness'. But if a 'y' is preceded by a vowel, the consonant remains — e.g. 'enjoy'/'enjoyment'.

Double or Quits

When adding a suffix to a word ending in a single consonant preceded by two vowels, you don't double the consonant — e.g. 'contain'/'containing'. But with words of one syllable containing a single final consonant after a single vowel, you do — e.g. 'hop'/'hopped', 'slop'/'slopping'. (If you didn't double that consonant, in those instances you would change the very meaning of the words — i.e. 'hoping' and 'sloping'.) With words of one syllable ending with two consonants, or with two vowels together before a final consonant, you do not double the final consonant — e.g. 'sharp'/'sharper', 'fool'/'fooling'. With words of two or more syllables ending with a consonant, where the stress is on the final syllable (e.g. 'admit', 'begin', 'travel'), you double that final consonant when adding the suffix (e.g. 'admitted', 'beginning', 'traveller'). Of course, in America it's different — some of the time. There they have a double 'n' in 'beginner' but only one 'l' in 'traveler' — which is why I reckon the next rule is more useful than the four you have just struggled through.

5. Think about the Word You Need to Spell

Break the Word Down

Divide the word into its component parts and work through the spelling of one part at a time. 'Fore-see-able' — no problem. 'Dis-com-bob-u-late' — easy. 'Tin-tin-abulation' — getting the idea? 'Pneumonoultramicro-scopicsilicovolcanoconiosis' — fuck off! No, hold on, it's the longest word in the dictionary; it's the name of a lung disease contracted from the inhalation of very fine silica particles, specifically from a volcano; and if you break it down into its constituent parts you can master the spelling quite easily. 'Pneu-mono-ultra-micro-scopic-silico-volcano-coni-osis.' There! Done! Hooray!

Say the Word out Loud

Say the word out loud, enunciating it as clearly as you can until it sounds right. It's 'Feb-ru-ary', not 'Febrary'; it's 'cemetery' not 'cematry'; it's 'se-cre-tary' not 'secraty'.

Create a Mnemonic

Mnemosyne means 'remembrance' in Greek and, in ancient Greek mythology, Mnemosyne was the goddess of memory. A 'mnemonic' is a device to help you remember something. If you want to recall the names of the first three men on the moon, it's as easy as ABC:

A — Neil **A**rmstrong
B — **B**uzz Aldrin
C — Michael **C**ollins

Given the vagaries of English spelling, and the fact that each and every spelling 'rule' is hedged about with exceptions, I am inclined to think that the best way to improve your spelling is to work out which are the words you always seem to get wrong and then create a mnemonic for each of them to ensure that, in future, you get them right. Mnemonics work by helping your brain encode and recall important information. They are a shortcut enabling you to associate the information you need to remember with a special word or phrase or acronym or image.

You will know the words you most often get wrong. (If you don't, watch out for them and make a list.) I know the words that bedevil me. 'Apparently' is my worst. I can never remember if it's one 'p' or two and whether or not there's supposed to be a third 'a' in there instead of an 'e'. My mnemonic for 'apparently' is this:

'Apparently' is the Daddy of all spelling challenges —
'Ap' is a Welsh patronymic and my wife
was born in Wales —
Add 'Ap' to 'parent' and I'm there: apparently!

That may seem complicated to you. For me, it works every time. The most effective mnemonics are usually the most personal: the ones that you have devised and that you know work for you. Here is a list of the 111 British English words that, according to a variety of surveys, most people misspell most often. Weird that 'weird' was top of the list when it's bottom here. It's top of the list because it is the most frequently misspelled word; 'separate' and 'accommodate' tied in second place. It's last in my list because I have listed the words alphabetically. For each one, I have added a mnemonic of sorts. Some are traditional; some are my own creation. If there are words here that you frequently find challenging, either use my mnemonic or have fun devising your own. The letters in **bold** are the ones that should help you avoid the mistakes most people most make with these words. With 'accelerator', is it one 'c' or two, one 'l' or two? Is it 'accessible' or 'accessable'?

1. Accelerator
   I met **a cruel creature** on the escal**ator**

2. Accessible
   I caught **a cruel creature** hi**ss**ing at my b**ible**

3. Accidentally
   A cruel creature my **dent**ist and certainly not
   my **ally**

4. Accommodation
   Accommodation offering **c**omfortable **c**hairs
   or modern **m**attresses **or** ... Think of the
   accommodation being so generous it includes
   two 'a's, two 'c's, two 'm's and three 'o's

5. Achieve
   I before **e** to ach**ie**ve success

6. Across
   Carry **a cross** across a crowded room

7. Address
   Directly **d**elivered letters arrive **s**afe and **s**ound

8. Aeroplane
   All **e**ngines **r**unning **ok**ay

9. Aggression/aggressive
   Wild horses get you there: gee-gees with
   two 'g's

10. Allege
    All — for example, **e.g.** — e

11. Apparently
A Welsh father: **ap parent**

12. Appearance
Mind your appearance when you make your ent**rance** at the d**ance**

13. Argument
Gummo Marx lost one 'e' in an ar**gum**ent...
Groucho said, '**A r**ude **g**irl **u**ndresses — **my**
eyes need **t**aping'

14. Arithmetic
A rat in the house **m**ay **e**at the **i**ce
cream

15. Assassination
Four killer words: **Ass — ass — I — nation**

16. Asthma
One cause of asthma: **s**ensitivity **t**o **h**ousehold
mites

17. Autumn
November comes at the end before winter
sets in

18. Avocado
O, o, av**o**cado!

19. Basically
Fundamental friend: **basic ally**

20. Beautiful
Big **e**lephants **are u**sually **beau**tiful

21. Because
   Big **e**lephants **c**an't **a**lways **u**se **s**mall **e**xits

22. Beginning
   It's easy to remember it's double 'n', because
   you propose at the begi**nn**ing, down on two
   knees

23. Belief/believe
   Never be**lie**ve a **lie**

24. Biscuit
   Bis cuit is French for 'twice cooked'

25. Bizarre
   As bizarre as **Zorro** with one 'z' and two 'r's

26. Broccoli
   Broccoli is good for you and never **c**auses
   col**i**c … Cubby Broccoli gave us the Bond
   films – 007, double **'o'**, double **'c'** Broccoli, one
   'l' of a guy

27. Business/busy
   Get on the **bus** — you need to get **bus**y and
   be about your **bus**iness

28. Calendar
   Dara checked the calen**dar** every day

29. Caribbean
   Three words: **carib, bean** — Caribbean!

30. Cemetery
   Eileen found herself at 'e's in the cem**e**tery

31. Chaos
   Cyclones, hurricanes **and o**ther **s**torms create
   chaos

32. Character
   Charlotte's **act** is **erotic**

33. Chauffeur
   FFS, it's a French word – the **EU** is involved

34. Colleague
   I was in the same **league** as the coll**eague**
   I met at **college**

35. Coming
   Come quick – there's only time for one '**m**'

36. Committee
   Many **m**eetings **t**ake **t**ime — everyone's
   exhausted

37. Completely
   Make sure it's **complete** before you add the '**ly**'

38. Conscience
   Con science like Dr Frankenstein and you,
   too, will have a conscience

39. Correspondence
   Correct your **corre**spon**dence** in the **den**

40. Curiosity
   Curiosity made me curious about your **curios**

41. Definitely
   There's a **finite** answer to this – de**finite**ly

42. Deliberate
It was a deliberate plan to **liberate Liberac**e

43. Desperate
Desperate **despera**dos!

44. Diarrhoea
Dash **in a r**eal **r**ush — hurry, **or e**lse accident!

45. Dilemma
Emma faced a dil**emma**

46. Disappear
Do I suddenly appear? No!

47. Doubt
It's only natural to **be** in dou**bt**

48. Ecstasy
Eric Clapton **s**tood **t**all **a**nd **s**aid **'Yes!'**

49. Eczema
It's not X-rated: **even clean zea**lots **ma**y get eczema

50. Embarrass
It's hard to emba**rrass r**eally **r**ighteous **a**nd **s**erious **s**tudents, though some **r**eally **r**edden **a**nd **s**mile **sh**yly when emba**rrass**ed

51. Environment
We need to **iron** out these env**iron**mental issues

52. Exaggerate
You double up when you exa**gg**erate — and

I've been caught bra**gg**ing when I've done well
on the **gee-g**ees

53. Existence
Eee, but it's easy, you just have to exist

54. Familiar
That **liar** looks fam**iliar**

55. Fascinate
Science is fa**sci**nating

56. Finally
Two words: **fin, ally** — finally

57. Fluorescent
Peter Pan **flu o'** the **c**rescent

58. Foreign
The Fo**reign** Office's heyday was in Queen
Victoria's **reign**

59. Foreseeable
At the **fore** of the ship is where you're **able**
to **see** most

60. Forty
Forget the 'u' when you hit forty

61. Friend
Have a **frie**d egg with a **frie**nd

62. Fulfil
One 'l' of a word: it's **full** and **fill** with just
one 'l' in each

63. Generally
Generally speaking, a **general** is your best
ally

64. Gist
Gist is a **gi**ft of a word

65. Government
The **govern**ment **govern**s

66. Grammar
To **ram** it home, remember Grand**ma** whose
g**ramma**r is always good

67. Guard
Go **u**ndercover **a**nd **r**einforce **d**efences

68. Handkerchief
A handkerchief is the **kerchief** you hold in
your **hand** (and a hanky is shorter and easy to
remember because hanky-panky is what
happens when **d**ad's not there)

69. Harass, harassment
Harold the **ass**
Made a pass

70. Honorary
A prophet is without honour in his own
country, and **honor** is without a 'u' in
America

71. Humorous
It's humorous the way Americans spell **humor**

72. Idiosyncrasy
O, it's **i,i,y,y,s,s** — it's sort of **crazy** — it's id**iosyncrasy**

73. Immediately
It's right now — it's **immediate** — and then you add 'ly'

74. Incidentally
After the **incident** you'll need an **ally**

75. Independent
Once you're **in**, easy does it (with three 'e's)

76. Indispensable
The chemist **dispens**es medicines **ably**

77. Interrupt
Grr — it's really **r**ude to inter**r**upt

78. Irresistible
'**I**', '**i**', you can't really **resist** me: I'm **irresisti**ble

79. Island
An island **is land** surrounded by water.

80. Jewellery
In Britain it's the jeweller who makes jewellery — but in the US you're short-changed: the jeweler there is one 'l' of a guy and he makes jewelry

81. Jodhpurs
Jodhpurs came from Jodhpur in India and you won't forget the '**h**' because you wear them

when **horse-riding**. (And that '**h**' comes before the '**p**' just as slipping out of your jodhpurs should come before you pee.)

82. Knowledge
Get your knowledge off the shelf — or **ledge**: don't lose your intellectual **edge**

83. Liaison
'**I**', '**i**', this looks like a dangerous liaison

84. Lollipop
I love lollipops (y not!)

85. Manoeuvre
O '**e** of little faith: **man**, just remember *oeuvre* is the French word for a work of some kind

86. Memento
Memo to self: it's got nothing to do with the moment that is now and everything to do with **reme**mbering happy **mem**ories of the past

87. Millennium
A **millennium** is a thousand years — it's a big number and calls for the max: two '**m**'s, two '**i**'s, two '**l**'s, two '**n**'s

88. Miniature
Here's looking **at u** in your **mini**

89. Mississippi
It's a big river, double the size of most: double-'s', double-'s', double-'p', or **Miss is sipp**ing Mississippi water.

90. Misspell
Miss Pell never **misspell**s

91. Necessary
This word is the pits: remember the **cess**pool
at its centre — or think of a shirt that has one
collar and two **s**leeves

92. Noticeable
You're on **notice**: you should be **able** to get
this right

93. Occasion
You'd cross two 'c's for a special occasion

94. Occurrence, occurred
E, **R**ed **R**um's disappearance was a **r**ight **r**um
occu**rr**ence

95. Parallel
Just one pair of para**ll**el bars in the middle of
this word

96. Parliament
Parliament — home of the big '**I am**'s!

97. Pavilion
Pavi the **lion** was on display in the
pavilion

98. Persistent
Keep going until you reach the **tent**

99. Pneumonia
People **n**ever **ex**pect **u** to get pneumonia

100. Portuguese
Don't be a goose: go as a **gue**st when you go
to Portugal

101. Possession
Your sweetest possession? A po**ss**et with
four **s**ugar**s**

102. Quiet
Please keep qu**iet** about my d**iet**

103. Receive
It's better to **g**ive than to rece**ive**

104. Rhythm
Rhythm **h**elps **y**our **t**wo **h**ips **m**ove

105. Separate
Don't forget: there's **a rat** in sep**arat**e

106. Siege
'**I**' before '**e**' when it rhymes with 'bee'

107. Subtle
Be subtle: **b** silent

108. Supersede
Supersede has not been superseded. There's no
other word in the English language that ends
with -sede

109. Truly
It's tr**uly** hot in **July**

110. Wednesday
If Friday is fish day, Wednesday is **We do not
eat soup day**

111. Weird
Eee, aye, adio — w**ei**rd or what?
It's **'e'**, **'i'** in w**ei**rd or you're a clot!

Is Alright Okay?

I'm not sure that it is.

When I asked the distinguished theatre director Sir Peter Hall why he had been married so many times, he said simply: 'When it's not all right, it's all wrong.' As a diminutive of 'all right' 'alright' feels all wrong to me. Several respectable dictionaries reckon it's acceptable nowadays. I don't. The Brandreth Rule is: avoid 'alright'. All right?

That said, there are other instances where two words are brought into one that are wholly acceptable in my book. Whether you use them as two words, or one, depends on what you are trying to say.

All together — altogether
All together now: 'Happy birthday to you...'
I've had six slices of birthday cake altogether

Any one — anyone
Any one of you can wish me a happy birthday
Anyone can come to the party — I don't care

All ways — always

All ways lead to death in the end
Always look on the bright side of life

Can not — cannot

You can not be serious! [with emphasis]
You cannot be serious … [with less emphasis]
You can not speak Urdu — you don't know the language
You cannot speak Urdu — it's not allowed

Every day — everyday

Every day we have a party here
A party here is an everyday occurrence

Every one — everyone

Every one of them is happy
Everyone is happy

In to — into

I can't get in to this party — I've not been invited
I can't get into the room
I've got into the room — I've got in to the party — but
I don't seem to be able to get 'into' the vibe

May be — maybe

It may be May, but it feels like March
Maybe tomorrow will be warmer
[may be = could be; maybe = perhaps[17]]

---

[17] When I was a boy, I was taught that 'maybe' wasn't a very nice word. You could get away with it in conversation, just, but never in

No one — no one
'Noone' is WRONG
'No-one' is okay (just) but BEST AVOIDED
'No one' is CORRECT

Some body — somebody
No body — nobody
Any body — anybody
There's some body lying in a pool of blood — will
somebody call the ambulance?
There's no body here now — nobody knows
what happened
Will any body do? If so, anybody can lend me a hand

Some times — sometimes
Some times are better than others — and
tonight's not good
Sometimes I'm just not in the mood, that's all

Three into Two Will Go

You should write:

heretofore as **heretofore**
nevertheless as **nevertheless**
notwithstanding as **notwithstanding**

'good' writing. Perhaps that's still true. Or maybe not. Possibly I'm
behind the times on this one.

whatsoever, **whosoever, wheresoever**
and **howsoever** as
whatsoever, **whosoever, wheresoever**
and **howsoever**

But you can write:

forasmuch as **for as much**[18]
insofar as **in so far**
insomuch as **in so much**

And these days – when I would accept 'newspaperman' for 'newspaper man' and some authorities approve 'plain-clothesman' for 'plain clothes man' — you can even get away with:

thingamajig
thingamabob
whatchamacallit

A 'thingamajig' (made up of 'thing' with a nonsense suffix) and a 'thingamabob', as words for something you've forgotten, have been around since at least the 1820s. The 'whatchamacallit' (what-you-may-call-it) came onto the scene exactly a hundred years later. As Noël Coward sagely

---

[18] But, to me, it feels better as just one word — as in the great line from the Rites of Burial in the Book of Common Prayer: 'Forsasmuch as it hath pleased Almighty God, in his wise providence, to take out of this world the soul of our deceased brother, we therefore commit his body to the ground; earth to earth, ashes to ashes, dust to dust...'

observed when he discovered that the Pacific island of Pago Pago is pronounced 'Pango Pango' and is only so called because the map-maker was short of 'n's at the time: 'You live and learn and then, of course, you die and forget it all.'

The Silent English Alphabet

One of the reasons that English spelling can be challenging is that a good number of words contain letters that need to be there when written, but aren't pronounced when spoken — e.g. 'psalm', 'psychology', and 'pterodactyl', where, you'll recall from the old joke, 'the p is silent — as in swimming pool'.

These silent letters are there mostly for historical reasons: they might have been pronounced in eras gone by; or they might have come to us from other languages in which they are pronounced, though they are not in ours. For example, we have chosen to pronounce the Japanese word 'tsunami' as 'sunami' simply because we are not familiar with English words that begin with the letters 'ts'.

Some of these silent letters are there for a purpose. Known as 'diacritic letters' they are present, not to be pronounced themselves, but to affect the pronunciation of another syllable. For example, when you add an 'e' to the letters 'f', 'a', 't', you don't pronounce the word as 'fat-ee' but as 'fate'. We don't hear that 'e', but it's what turns your 'fat' into your 'fate'.

Back in 1969, the Association of Teachers of English to Speakers of Other Languages debated how to correctly pronounce the association's acronym, TESOL.

Eventually, they decided it would be amusing to do it with letters drawn from a 'silent alphabet', with a 'T' as in 'castle', an 'E' as in 'give', an 'S' as in 'island', an 'O' as in 'people', and an 'L' as in 'calm'.

Here is my 'silent alphabet'. If you are able to add to it, feel free. And if you can come up with words for the letters 'J', and 'V', please tweet them to me (@GylesB1) so that they (and you) can feature in future editions. Some people would include 'marijuana' under 'J', but I wouldn't, because even though the 'j' isn't pronounced as a 'j', it *is* pronounced as an 'h', so it isn't, strictly speaking, a silent letter.

The silent letters are in **bold**:

A: **a**esthetic, brea**d**, hea**d**
B: de**b**t, dum**b**er, plum**b**er
C: indi**c**tment, mus**c**le, s**c**ience
D: han**d**kerchief, We**d**nesday
E: fat**e**, fin**e**, giv**e**, lik**e**, nam**e**
F: hal**f**penny
G: **g**nat, **g**naw, hi**gh**, phle**g**m, si**g**n, thou**gh**
H: daug**h**ter, ec**h**o, **h**eir,[19] **h**onest, **h**our, orc**h**id
I: bus**i**ness, fr**i**end
K: **k**nee, **k**nife, **k**night, **k**not, **k**now
L: ca**l**f, cou**l**d, ta**l**k, yo**l**k

---

[19] As a party trick, I sometimes ask friends to say the words 'heir', 'hair', and 'lair' out loud one after the other. Give it a go: 'heir, hair, lair'. You'll sound as lah-di-dah as I do, instantly. (To sound Australian, the three words you need are 'good', 'eye', 'might'.)

M: **m**ne**m**onic
N: autum**n**, colum**n**, dam**n**, hym**n**, solem**n**
O: c**o**lonel, le**o**pard, pe**o**ple
P: cor**p**s, cou**p**, **p**neumonia, recei**p**t
Q: lac**q**uer [I think we can get away with that
   one — just]
R: fo**r**ecastle, sa**r**saparilla
S: ai**s**le, debri**s**, i**s**land, i**s**le
T: balle**t**, cas**t**le, rappor**t**, lis**t**en
U: colleag**u**e, g**u**ard, g**u**ess, tong**u**e
W: ans**w**er, s**w**ord, t**w**o, **w**rist, **w**rong
X: billet-dou**x** [French, I know, but we can get away
   with it, can't we?]
Y: gre**y**, tra**y** [or if you think you can hear the hint
   of a 'y' sound at the end of the those, I bring you
   the name 'Pepys']
Z: rende**z**vous

Capital Idea

As I probably don't need to tell you, 'Capital Letters' is the
title of a song from the soundtrack of the 2018 movie,
Fifty Shades Freed, the third film in the *Fifty Shades of Grey*
trilogy, which contains the message, I'm going to give it to
you 'in capital letters'. Cole Porter wrote all his stuff on his
own, but this song had *six* writers and it seems it's true
that nothing succeeds like excess because the movie in
which the song features, while panned by the critics,
grossed six times its budget of $55 million within six

weeks of opening. *Gay Times* called the song 'a total banger' — and meant it as a compliment.

When it comes to giving it to you in capital letters, these are the rules:

Use a capital letter ...

- for the first word of a sentence.
- for the first word in a line of song lyrics or in poetry — unless the poet wants it otherwise.[20]
- for the first word and the significant words in the titles of books, films, plays, etc., but only the significant words, so that it is *Fifty Shades of Grey*, not *Fifty Shades Of Grey*, *The Catcher in the Rye* not *The Catcher In The Rye*, *Romeo and Juliet* not *Romeo And Juliet*.[21]
- for names and proper nouns (unless it's k.d. lang — there's no point in being difficult) — e.g. 'Christian Grey' and 'Anastasia Steele', and 'the Queen', 'the President', and holders of different

---

[20] The American poet E. E. Cummings (1894–1962) wrote most of his poetry using lower case letters, but it is a myth that he insisted on having his name written as 'e e cummings'. He signed his name using upper and lower case letters in the customary way. (The phrases 'upper case' and 'lower case' come from the early days of printing, when typesetting involved individual letters; the most frequently used letters were stored in the more accessible lower case of letters and the capital letters stored in the upper case.)

[21] ''Twas in a restaurant they met, / Romeo and Juliet. / 'Twas there he first got into debt, / Rome-owed what Juli-et.'

offices, when referring to a specific individual. When referring to the role rather than the person, lower case is used — e.g. 'the Queen is both a queen and a mother,' said the Prince of Wales, who is both a prince and a son. 'Her Majesty is much looking forward to meeting President Trump. She has met so many presidents, she doesn't feel her majesty will be in any way diminished by the encounter.'

- for place names and the names of buildings — e.g. 'New York' and 'the Empire State Building'.
- for adjectives derived from proper nouns — e.g. 'Scandinavian' and 'Shakespearean'.
- for days of the week, months of the year, and special days — e.g. 'Monday', 'Tuesday', 'January', 'February', 'Easter', 'Christmas', 'Valentine's Day'. But not, curiously, for the seasons: they are always 'spring', 'summer', 'autumn', and 'winter'.
- for eras in history (e.g. 'the Dark Ages', 'the Swinging Sixties')' but not for specific times (e.g. 'the fifteenth century').
- for God when it is the Almighty, but not for gods in general — e.g. 'Allah be praised!'; 'the gods smiled on us'.
- for the pronoun 'I'.
- for most letters in words that are acronyms — e.g. 'the EU', 'NATO', 'NASA'. But not where the acronym has become a word in its own right — e.g. 'scuba', which is short for 'Self-Contained

Underwater Breathing Apparatus'; or 'radar', which comes from 'Radio Detection and Ranging'. Some style guides now advocate only using capitals throughout for acronyms where the letters are individually pronounced — e.g. they would capitalise all of 'BBC' and 'EU' but only the first letters in 'Nato' or 'Nasa'. Because it's what now happens, I accept it, but I do not approve. I think putting each letter in capitals is a useful reminder that it is part of an acronym.

- for brand names when they are being used as brand names — e.g. 'Hoover', 'Google'. But not when they are being used as verbs, as in: 'When I had finished hoovering, I googled "Mars" and discovered that the chocolate Mars bar isn't named after the planet Mars, but after Forrest Mars, the confectioner who invented it.'
- for the names of languages — e.g. English, French, Hindi, Gujarati, Esperanto. But not, interestingly, for the names of academic disciplines or school subjects, unless they happen to be languages — e.g. 'At school I studied history, geography, and maths, as well as Latin, French, and Greek.'
- for words that are used to show a connection with a particular place — e.g. 'Dutch Old Masters', 'the French negotiators', 'the Russian Revolution'. But not when those words don't refer exclusively to the place in question — e.g. it can be 'dutch courage', a 'french letter', and

'russian salad'. This is controversial, and different authorities take different lines, but I go along with my old mentor, the late Larry Trask, Professor of Linguistics at the University of Sussex: 'Words that express a connection with a particular place must be capitalised when they have their literal meanings. So, for example, "French" must be capitalised when it means "having to do with France"... However, it is not necessary to capitalise these words when they occur as parts of fixed phrases and don't express any direct connection with the relevant places: for example, "Please buy some danish pastries"; "in warm weather, we keep our french windows open"; "I prefer russian dressing on my salad".' Why the difference? Well, a danish pastry is merely a particular sort of pastry; it doesn't have to come from Denmark. Likewise, french windows are merely a particular kind of window, and russian dressing is just a particular variety of salad dressing. Even in these cases, you can capitalise these words if you want to, as long as you are consistent about it. But notice how convenient it can be to make the difference: 'In warm weather, we keep our french windows open'; 'After nightfall, French windows are always shuttered.' In the first example, 'french windows' just refers to a kind of window; in the second, 'French windows' refers specifically to windows in France.

The Brandreth Rule is: don't take capital letters for granted. They make a difference. 'Helping my uncle jack off his horse' is not at all the same as 'Helping my Uncle Jack off his horse', is it?

5. Of Mice & Meece & Mouses

We'll begin with a box, and the plural is boxes,
But the plural of ox becomes oxen, not oxes;
Then one fowl is a goose, but two are called geese,
Yet the plural of mouse should never be meese.
You may find a lone mouse or a nest full of mice,
Yet the plural of house is houses, not hice.

If the plural of man is always called men,
Why shouldn't the plural of pan be called pen? ...

If I speak of a foot and you show me your feet,
And I give you a boot, would a pair be called beet?
If one is a tooth, and a whole set are teeth,
Why shouldn't the plural of booth be called beeth? ...
Then one may be that, and three would be those,
Yet hat in the plural would never be hose,
And the plural of cat is cats, not cose.

We speak of a brother and also of brethren,
But though we say mother, we never say methren:
Then the masculine pronouns are he, his and him,
But imagine the feminine: she, shis and shim ...

Pluralizing English is a singular business. There is an explanation for most (if not all) of the apparently illogical

discrepancies between one plural and another and it is to do with where the root words come from. The reason, for example, that the plural of 'ox' is 'oxen' is that both words have come down to us from Anglo-Saxon, the Old English language derived from a West Germanic language and spoken in large parts of England and southern Scotland between the fifth and twelfth centuries. Our modern vocabulary includes thousands of words of Anglo-Saxon descent, from 'axe' and 'aye' to 'you' and 'yelp',[22] via such favourites as 'buxom', 'buttock', 'frowzy', and 'fuck'. Other than 'oxen', only two other plural nouns in modern English end the same way: 'children' and 'brethren'. Once, other nouns like 'eye' and 'house' were pluralised as 'eyen' and 'housen'. The plural of 'hose' used to be 'hosen' and, happily, German *lederhosen* are still being worn to remind us of the old Germanic link.

There's a Germanic explanation for why we get 'geese' from 'goose' and 'feet' from 'foot', as well. Because they change in form these are known as 'mutated plurals' and

---

[22] But you can't do an A to Z of Anglo-Saxon words that have come down to modern English. There are none beginning with 'x' or 'z', and apart from 'vane', 'vat', and 'vixen', none that I know of beginning with 'v'. Among the 'y' words is one of my favourites: 'yex'. It means a 'hiccup' or 'belch' and is a very useful word to play in a tight corner at Scrabble. 'Hiccup', incidentally, is the correct spelling and variants of it — 'hickop', 'hyckock', 'hicket' — have been around since before Shakespeare was born in 1564. Like the French *hoquet*, the word imitates the sound of a hiccup. The spelling 'hiccough' came along shortly after Shakespeare's death in 1616; but as a hiccup has no anatomical connection with a cough, it should not have caught on and, nowadays, is taboo. The word 'hiccup', incidentally, replaced the Old English word, 'ælfsogoða', so called because hiccups were thought to be caused by elves.

the mutation involves changing the vowel sound of the singular word in a process called *umlaut*. This *umlaut* is not to be confused with the *umlaut* that is the double-dot mark (¨) used over a vowel, especially in German, to indicate a different vowel quality — though it's not unconnected. This *umlaut* is the name of the linguistic process that changes the way we say and spell certain words of Anglo-Saxon origin when we pluralise them – e.g.:

foot — feet
goose — geese
louse — lice
man — men
mouse — mice
tooth — teeth
woman — women

NB. The plural of 'mouse' is always 'mice'. Americans of a certain generation are under the misapprehension that 'meece' may be acceptable. This is thanks to a Hanna-Barbera television cartoon series, *Pixie and Dixie and Mr Jinks*, which featured as a regular segment of *The Huckleberry Hound Show* from 1958 to 1961. The series, in the tradition of *Tom and Jerry*, featured two young mice, Pixie and Dixie, and their bow-tied feline nemesis, Mr Jinks, whose voice was modelled on that of the actor Marlon Brando, and whose oft-repeated catchphrase was: 'I hates those meeces to pieces!' The plural of the computer 'mouse', however, while it can be 'mice', is more usually 'mouses'.

When referring to other animals, the plural of 'moose' is 'moose', just as the plurals of 'deer', 'fish', 'sheep', and 'swine' are 'deer', 'fish, 'sheep', and 'swine'. This is because the words already count as collective nouns of a kind. 'Fish', however, is a little different from the rest, because there are occasions when the word 'fishes' as a plural noun is acceptable, e.g.:

> There are six fish in the pond.
> There are fishes of all kinds in the lake.

Mistakenly, some authorities permit 'fishies' as a plural of fish. This dates back to the song, 'Three Little Fishies', which became a Number One hit in the US in 1939, recorded by Kay Kyser and his Orchestra, and popular in the UK from 1949, when it was recorded by the comedian Frankie Howerd. 'Fishies' is definitely fishy. Stick with 'fish'.

There is no escaping the fact that the world of plurals is full of spelling challenges. Having got 'potatoe' wrong, it could be that Vice-President Dan Quayle would have got the plural, 'potatoes', right. But why is 'potatos' and 'tomatos' wrong, when 'avocados' is right? Good question. There's no good answer. Sometimes you just have to take what you're given and live with it. The word 'bus' comes from the Latin 'omnibus': the plural can be 'buses' or 'busses'. The bus may end up in the terminus. The word 'terminus' comes from the Latin, too, but the plural of 'terminus' can be 'terminuses' or 'termini', but never 'terminusses'. It's confusing, but I am here to help.

Happily, most nouns make their plurals just by adding an 's' to the end of the word — so that 'noun' becomes 'nouns' and 'word' becomes 'words'.

But some, of course, do change their endings.

Nouns Ending in '-y'

If the noun ends with a consonant plus a 'y', make the plural by changing the 'y' to 'ies' — e.g.:

city — cities
cherry — cherries
calamity — calamities

Nouns Ending in 'ch', 's', 'sh', 'x', or 'z'

If the noun ends with 'ch', 's', 'sh', 'x', or 'z', add 'es' to form the plural:

bus — buses
church — churches
quiz — quizzes
tax — taxes
wish — wishes

But hold on. What's with the extra 'z' in 'quizzes'? Where's that come from? It's come from a good general rule that words should be spelled in such a way that they *sound* right. 'Quizes' with one 'z' would sound wrong because normally we pronounce 'ize' to rhyme with 'eyes' not 'is'. Add that extra 'z' and 'quizzes' sounds as it should. For the same reason, some authorities allow you to spell 'buses' with a double 's'. (As my cousin from South Carolina exclaimed when I told him this: 'Kiss my bus! Is that a fact?') My friend, Samuel West, the distinguished actor, told me that he had come across the old word 'buss' (meaning 'kiss') in an audiobook he was reading and as a consequence decided one good reason to spell 'the big red thing with one "s"' is to avoid confusion about which one might be along in a minute'.

And with words ending in 'ch' there is a special exception here that's worth noting. As a rule, words that end with a 'ch' require the plural 'es' (e.g. 'witches', 'watches', 'batches', 'bitches'); but if the 'ch' ending is pronounced with a 'k' sound, you just add a solitary 's':

epoch — epochs
monarch — monarchs
stomach — stomachs

Nouns Ending in 'f' or 'fe'

With nouns that end in a consonant or a single vowel plus 'f' or 'fe', change the 'f' or 'fe' to 'ves':

calf — calves
knife — knives
sheaf — sheaves
shelf — shelves
wife — wives

Once upon a time (up until the beginning of the twentieth century), the plural of 'roof' and 'hoof' would have been 'rooves' and 'hooves'. Now, 'rooves', though still technically allowable, is regarded as archaic and best avoided, but 'hooves' has not been totally replaced by 'hoofs': you can use either. The same goes for 'halfs' and 'halves', 'scarfs' and 'scarves', and 'wharfs' and 'wharves'. And when it comes to 'Snow White and the Seven Dwarfs' or 'Snow White and the Seven Dwarves', either used to go, but now neither is really allowable. We prefer 'Snow Green and the Seven Persons of Restricted Growth'. The plural of 'elf', however, is always 'elves' and never 'elfs'.

Nouns which end in two vowels plus 'f' mostly form plurals in the normal way, with just an 's' added:

belief — beliefs
chief — chiefs
grief — griefs
oaf — oafs
spoof — spoofs

I said 'mostly'. I didn't say 'always'. The plural of 'chief' is always 'chiefs', but the plural of 'handkerchief' can be either 'handkerchiefs' or 'handkerchieves'. And while 'thief' sounds and looks and *is* so like 'chief', it's always 'Ali Baba and the Forty Thieves'. 'Oaf' and 'loaf' seem similar, too, but nonetheless when it comes to the plurals it's 'oafs and fools' and 'loaves and fishes'.

I was about to say that in the case of 'leaf' the plural is always 'leaves', and then I remembered that my mother, my daughter, and one of my grandsons have all lived in Toronto and supported the 'Maple Leafs' hockey team.

Nouns Ending in 'o'

Nouns ending in 'o' can be made plural with either an 's' or an 'es' and sometimes with either.

As a general rule, most nouns ending in 'o' add a single 's' to make the plural:

avocado — avocados
solo — solos
zero — zeros

Those which have a vowel before the final 'o' are ones where you always just add a single 's':

rodeo — rodeos
studio — studios
zoo — zoos

But with a number of nouns ending in 'o', 'es' is always added in the plural, *viz*:

buffalo — buffaloes
domino — dominoes
echo — echoes
embargo — embargoes
hero — heroes
mosquito — mosquitoes
potato — potatoes
torpedo — torpedoes
veto — vetoes

Why is the plural of 'hero' 'heroes' and the plural of 'zero' 'zeros'? Nobody knows. It's just the way it is. And you might as well go with the flow if you don't want to look like an ignorant oik.

Sometimes, for no good reason either, you get a choice:

banjo — banjos or banjoes
cargo — cargos or cargoes
flamingo — flamingos or flamingoes
fresco — frescos or frescoes
ghetto — ghetto or ghettoes
halo — halos or haloes
mango — mangos or mangoes
memento — mementos or mementoes
motto — mottos or mottoes
tornado — tornados or tornadoes
volcano — volcanos or volcanoes

Nouns Derived from Latin

You get a choice, too, when it comes to the plurals of words that have come into English from Latin. You can opt for the Latin plural or the English.

	Latin plural	English plural
antenna	antennae	antennas
appendix	appendices	appendixes
aquarium	aquaria	aquariums
cactus	cacti	cactuses
curriculum	curricula	curriculums
formula	formulae	formulas
index	indices	indexes
millennium	millennia	millenniums
referendum	referenda	referendums
stadium	stadia	stadiums
terminus	termini	terminuses
thesaurus	thesauri	thesauruses
vortex	vortices	vortexes

My Latin is not good, so I'm not consistent when it comes to my plurals. I say 'stadia' rather than 'stadiums', but 'aquariums' rather than 'aquaria'. What I do know is that there are just a few Latin words in the English language where only the Latin plural is allowed, e.g.:

alga — algae
alumnus — alumni
larva — larvae

Conversely, the plural of 'octopus' is always 'octopuses' and never 'octopi'. Why? Because, though 'octopus' is a Latin scientific name, it comes originally from the ancient Greek — which explains why, among Greek geeks, 'octopodes' as a plural for 'octopus' is sometimes used.

Nouns Derived from Greek

Nouns which end in 'is' often come from the Greek. Their plurals are made by changing the 'is' to 'es', e.g.:

analysis — analyses
crisis — crises
diagnosis — diagnoses

Nouns Derived from French

Certain words that have come into English from French have two possible plural forms: the original French plural and an English one. For example, the plural of 'bureau' can be the French plural 'bureaux' or the English 'bureaus'. The same goes for 'chateaux' and 'chateaus' and 'gateaux' and 'gateaus'. If you spell the plural with the English plural, you should pronounce it in the English way, too. You eat *'gato'* in *'Pari'* but *'gattoes'* in Paris.

Nouns Derived from Italian

Most words which have come into English from Italian form their plurals with an 's', as if they were English words. For example, the Italian plural of *cappuccino* is *cappuccini*, but when the word is used in English, its plural form is 'cappuccinos'. That's why the plural of *espresso* isn't *espressi* but 'espressos'; more than one *pizza* aren't *pizze*, they're 'pizzas'. That said, if you have more than one *paparazzo* on your tail, not only do you have my sympathy, I am also here to tell you that the plural of *paparazzo* in English is the same as it is in Italian: 'paparazzi'.

Spaghetti, tagliatelle, tortellini, cannelloni, scampi, and panini are already in their Italian plural forms, but when you are ordering them in English-speaking territories you can pluralise them with an extra 's': 'We'll have two tortellinis and three scampis, please.' In British English, we spell 'lasagne' with an 'e' at the end. In American English, it's spelled with an 'a' at the end. *Lasagna*, in fact, is the Italian singular form, though, curiously, it's rarely used in Italian.

Basta!

The good news is we're almost there — but not quite. There's still stuff we have to cover first.

Stuff

You can stuff your bag with stuff, not with 'stuffs'. 'Stuffs' exists as a verb, but not as a noun, except if you are referring to different types of cloth known as stuff. 'Stuff' is one of those nouns that's known in the grammar trade as **uncountable**. Uncountable nouns include stuff like 'stuff' that don't have a plural form because they are implicitly plural and cannot be divided. 'Sunshine', 'flour', 'sugar', 'milk', 'earth', 'water', 'happiness', 'truth', 'humour' are all uncountable nouns. As a rule, you cannot put an 'a' or an 'an' in front of them. You will hope for 'sunshine on Tuesday' or 'bursts of sunshine', but never 'a sunshine'. You go out to buy 'bottles of milk' or 'milk', but rarely 'milks' — unless, of course, they are specific ones: 'different flavoured milks'. If he had 'hair on his head', he had a head of hair. If he had 'hairs on his head', they were individual ones. If you can see the difference, you've mastered the mystery of uncountable nouns.

News

The French for 'news' is '*les nouvelles*' and it is plural. 'News', while it derives from 'new' and sounds like the plural of 'new', isn't. 'News' is a singular noun, which is why the newsreader says, 'Here is the news,' rather than 'Here are the news.' It's uncountable, too, which is why you might have 'good news' to share, or 'a piece of good news', but never 'a good news'.

Series

While we're in front of the TV, I should explain that 'series' is a singular noun, but it's not uncountable, and the plural of 'series' is 'series', too. That's why you need to use a singular verb when talking about just one series, but a plural when you are speaking of more than one — e.g. '*Frasier* was a favourite series of mine, but the various series with Kelsey Grammer that followed weren't so hot.'

Means and Beans

'Means' is both singular and plural, and countable, too — e.g. 'As a child, my tricycle was my favourite means of transport, but I realise there were other means of getting around.' Names of foods, while plural, are treated singularly when they are treated as a single dish — e.g. 'Baked beans is my favourite lunch and fried eggs for breakfast is best.'

Bellows, Tongs, Tights, and Thongs

A bellows is an instrument for blowing air. The plural of 'bellows' is 'bellows' and you use the singular verb if you're talking about just one bellows and the plural when there is more than one. Curiously, it's different with tongs. Tongs come in pairs, like scissors and tights and tweezers and jeans and trousers and spectacles and pliers, so they are used only in the plural. 'The bellows blows air into the fire. The tongs pick up lumps of sugar from the bowl. The bellows is black. The tights are red.' Thongs, unlike tongs, can be singular or plural. 'Thongs are my thing. Your thong is too thin.'

Measles and Mumps

Measles is a disease. So is mumps. They are uncountable nouns and, despite the 's' on the end, you should treat them as singular. 'Measles is common among children' is correct. 'Mumps are common among children' is not.

Politics

'Politics', 'social studies', 'ethics', 'mathematics', 'physics' may all end with an 's', but as branches of knowledge they are treated as singular. 'Mathematics rocks! Politics stinks!'

Data Specific

'Criteria', 'phenomena', 'memoranda', and 'media' are plural. Their singular forms are 'criterion', 'phenomenon', 'memorandum', and 'medium'.

'Data' is plural, but in English the singular form, 'datum', is hardly ever used. Opt instead for 'a piece of data'.

Twenty Questions

What is the plural of...

1. Magnum opus?
2. Scampi?
3. Attorney General?
4. Lord Lieutenant?
5. Sergeant Major?
6. Mother-in-law?
7. Editor-in-chief?
8. Court-martial?
9. Sum total?
10. Body politic?
11. Sleight-of-hand?
12. Jack-in-the-box?
13. Poet Laureate?
14. Professor Emeritus?
15. Curriculum vitae?
16. Persona non grata?
17. Coup d'état?
18. Agent provocateur?
19. Femme fatale?
20. Cul-de-sac?

Twenty Answers

1. *Magna opera.*
2. *Scampi* — not *scampus*. *Scampi* is the Italian plural of *scampo*, but in English, *scampi* is used as singular, plural, or uncountable.

3. *Attorney Generals* in the US, but *Attorneys General* in the UK — and for a reason. As with *solicitors general*, *postmasters general*, *secretaries general*, the *general* in these compounds originated not as a noun (like a military general) but as an adjective: *general* as opposed to *specific*.

4. *Lord Lieutenants* — because they are *lieutenants* representing the *lord* or sovereign.

5. *Sergeants Major* is allowed, but *Sergeant Majors* is preferred. With *Lieutenant General*, *Major General*, and *Field Marshal*, only *Lieutenant Generals*, *Major Generals*, and *Field Marshals* can be allowed.

6. *Mothers-in-law.*

7. *Editors-in-chief.*

8. *Courts-martial. Martial* here is the adjective for *military*, which is why *courts-martial* is preferred, but *court-martials* is also acceptable.

9. *Sums total.*

10. *Bodies politic.*

11. *Sleights-of-hand.*

12. *Jacks-in-the-box* — because it sounds better. *Johnnies-come-lately* and *sticks-in-the-mud* are also preferred.

13. *Poets Laureate* — because *Laureate* here serves as the adjective describing the poet adorned with a wreath of laurel leaves. But, of course, when it comes to *Nobel laureates*, it's different. Here *laureates* is the noun and *Nobel* describes them.

14. *Professors Emeriti.* When it's just one, two, or three of them, you can stick with one, two, or three *professors emeritus*, but when it's a whole congregation go for *professors emeriti*.

15. *Curricula vitae. Curriculum vitae* means 'course of life' in Latin. *Curricula vitarum* meaning 'courses of lives' is technically the correct full plural, but *curriculum vitae* is the one to opt for if you want the job and don't want to come over as a pretentious prick.

16. *Personae non gratae* is the right answer — but not necessarily the one to use. 'They are *persona non grata*' is a more comfortable way of expressing it.

17. *Coups d'état.* It's the *coups* (the blows) that are being pluralised. The state (*l'état*) remains single.

18. *Agents provocateurs* — because both the noun and the adjective take an 's' in the French.

19. *Femmes fatales. La même chose! Et encore* for *forces majeures.*

20. *Cul-de-sacs* or *culs-de-sacs. Cul-de-sac* comes from the French for 'bottom of the bag'. *Cul-de-sacs* is considered an acceptable plural in English, but *culs-de-sacs* is rather more *comme il faut.*

Nine Rules

Before we leave the world of plurals, we have to tackle the thorny issue of 'subject/verb agreement'. You what? It's easier than it sounds, if you remember the rules — and the exceptions to them.

What are the rules?

1. The key to it all this is this: subjects and verbs must agree in number, like so:

141

The *summer* **is** hot
The *summers* **were** hot
The *girl* **is** hot
The *guys* **are** hotter

(The *subjects* is these examples are in italic: the verbs are in **bold**.)

2. Don't be confused if words come between the subject and verb as they do not affect agreement:

    The *girl*, wearing several layers, **is** hot
    The *guys*, wearing pretty much nothing, **are** hotter

3. If two subjects are joined by 'and', they require a plural verb form:

    The *girl* and the *boy* **are** getting carried away

4. The verb remains singular if the two subjects separated by 'and' refer to the same thing:

    Fish and *chips* **is** my Friday treat

5. If one of the words 'each', 'every', or 'no' comes before the subject, the verb is singular:

    Each *person* **is expected** to behave properly
    Every *boy* and *girl* **is expected** to arrive prepared
    No *nonsense* **is going** to be tolerated

6. If the subjects are both singular and are connected by the words 'or', 'nor', 'neither/nor', 'either/or', or 'not only/but also', the verb is singular:

> Neither *Adam* nor *Eve* **is** responsible for what happened next, nor **is** the *apple* or the *snake*

7. If one subject is singular and one plural and the words are connected by the words 'or', 'nor', 'neither/nor', 'either/or', or 'not only/but also', you use the verb form of the subject that is nearest the verb:

> Either the *apples* or the *serpent* **is** responsible for what's happened
> Neither the *serpent* nor the *apples* **have** been seen since

8. Indefinite pronouns typically take singular verbs:

> *Everybody* **wants** to be understood

Except for the pronouns 'few', 'many', 'several', 'some', 'both' and 'all' which always take the plural form:

> *Some* **want** to be loved
> *Few* **want** to be feared

9. Collective nouns like 'government', 'team', 'flock', 'crowd', 'company', 'management' usually take a singular verb form:

The *government* **is doing** tremendously well
The *crowd* **is getting** restless
The *team* **sucks**

People often slip into using a plural verb with these sorts of collective nouns, but 'The *government* **are** useless' is WRONG. 'Members of the government are useless' is correct, but if it's the government as an entity it needs to be: 'The *government* **is** useless.'

According to Debbie le May, editor of *Quest*, the journal of the Queen's English Society, there are exceptions to this rule: 'Sports teams and the emergency services should be referred to in the plural, so "Arsenal have just signed a new player", and "Police are looking for a suspect…"'

I'm not sure that Debbie is right. *'Accrington Stanley* **isn't** what it used to be' sounds okay to me. And while 'the *police* **is** looking for a suspect' does sound awkward, 'the *Metropolitan Police* **is** looking for a suspect' doesn't.

6. Yanks Away

We Brits gave the Americans their language and they have kindly returned it to us, with improvements.

That's not strictly true, of course. Hundreds, if not thousands, of languages were spoken by the various peoples of North America long before the first English-speakers appeared on their continent towards the end of the sixteenth century. Today, according to the US Census Bureau, around 2.9 million US citizens identify themselves as American Indian or Alaskan Native, and, while more than 70 per cent of those say they only speak English at home, a Native North American language is spoken in the homes of nearly 15 per cent of them. Navajo is the most commonly spoken Native language in the US with nearly 170,000 speakers, ten times the numbers that speak the next two most popular Native languages: Yupik and Sioux.

During my gap year, I travelled across the US and met a young Native American from Arizona who taught me the only half-dozen Navajo words I know:

Ch'iidii
Diigis
Da'alzhin
Chxo'
Joozh
Leechaa'itsa'ii biyaazh

It wasn't until I repeated the words in the presence of his family that I discovered they did not mean what he had told me they meant. If you want to be obscene in Navajo, you can be now. *Leechaa'itsa'ii biyaazh* translates as 'son of a bitch'. The rest I leave to your imagination. They sort of sound like what they are.

According to Unesco (or, as I like to think of it, UNESCO), most of the indigenous American languages in North America are critically endangered, and many are extinct. I am afraid that we Europeans are to blame. Half a millennium before Christopher Columbus sailed the ocean blue in 1492, the Vikings went over for a quick look-see. Later, the Danish, Dutch, French, Germans, Swedish, Maltese, Russians, and Portuguese, as well as the Spanish, all had a go at claiming a share of the New World; but, from 1607, with the founding of the London Company in Jamestown, Virginia, the English colonisation of North America began and quickly took hold.

In 1620, the Pilgrim Fathers, on board the *Mayflower*, arrived in Massachusetts. In 1664, the English conquered New Amsterdam and renamed it New York — in honour not so much of the city of York as of the Duke of York (later James II). Having driven out the Dutch, the English drove out the Spanish and went on to beat the French during the French and Indian War from 1754. By the time the thirteen British colonies on the east coast declared their independence in 1776 and formed the United States of America, they were almost entirely English-speaking. With the Louisiana Purchase of 1803, New Orleans became part of the US and a great slew of people speaking French, Creole, and Cajun joined the party. And, as the country

TENNYSON

BREAK   BREAK   BREAK

AND THE STATELY SHIPS GO ON
TO THEIR HAVEN UNDER THE HILL
BUT OH) FOR THE TOUCH OF A VANISHED HAND
AND THE SOUND OF A VOICE THAT IS STILL.

NNYYNY

ign
asset ma

Account Number: **0000140256** Registered

Transaction

Distribution Transactions

Date	**Transaction**	**Investment**
30-Nov-10	Distribution	Ignis Balanced Gro

Please note that charges and remunerations information has pre
This statement has been prepared at trade date.

moved west, more Spanish speakers came on board. But the power was in the east and the leaders of the land were English-speakers with English forebears. English became the pre-eminent language of the New World.

Of the 325 million people in the USA today, coming up for 50 million speak a language other than English at home. Spanish speakers account for 30 million of the total. More than 45 million Americans claim German heritage, but fewer than a million now speak the language. Up until the US joined the First World War, around 6 per cent of the country's primary school children were taught German. It's often said that English only defeated German by a single vote to become the official language of the United States, in a 1795 Congressional debate. In fact, there is no 'official' language in the US. More than five hundred languages are spoken in the country overall. English, Spanish, and Chinese come top. German is tied in tenth place with Russian, with Arabic and Italian in close contention. In New Mexico, official documents have to be published in Spanish. In Louisiana, they have to be available in French. In Hawaii, though almost no one speaks Hawaiian, it is one of the official languages. In Alaska, twenty Native languages are regarded as 'official', though English is the one most people use.

That's the point: in the US, and increasingly around the world, English is the language most people use. And because of the power of the dollar, the universal availability of US television, and the impact of Hollywood, many more people on the planet use American English than British English.

The Brandreth Rule is: when in Rome, do as the Romans

do — speak English; and if you're British, do so with a British accent and spell your English the British way. That isn't always easy — particularly if you haven't worked out how to opt out of American English auto-correct when using Microsoft Word.

The differences between British and American spelling spring largely from the British tendency to hold on to the spellings of words it has absorbed from other languages, while American English, with the championship of Noah Webster and his followers, has modified the traditional English spelling to reflect the way words sound when they are spoken.

If you are writing to or for an American audience, use American spellings. Otherwise, in my view, don't. Globalisation is leading inevitably towards cultural homogenisation. I think it's nice to hang on to the little differences while we can. (If I'd said, 'It's neat to hang on to the little differences,' you might have thought I was American. If I'd said 'wee differences', you'd have known I was a Scot. That's what I mean: they are little differences, but they do tell a story.)

Different Spellings

Here are the big differences between British English spelling and American English spelling:

- **Words ending in *-re***

  British English words that end in *-re* mostly end in *-er* in American English:

British	US
centre	center
litre	liter
theatre	theater

• Words ending in *-ize* or *-ise*

In British English and American English, these words and all words ending with the suffix *-wise* (e.g. 'clockwise', 'otherwise') must always be spelled with the ending in *ise*:

advertise
advise
apprise
arise
chastise
circumcise
comprise
compromise
demise
despise
devise
disguise
enterprise
excise
exercise
franchise
guise
improvise

incise

merchandise

mortise

premise

reprise

revise

supervise

surmise

surprise

televise

None of the above can ever be spelled with an *-ize*. But lots of other words that I was brought up to spell with an *-ise* (e.g. civilise, finalise, memorise, patronise) can now be spelled in British English with an *-ize*. I don't like it, but you can do it if you want. You won't be wrong. In fact, in this instance, you will be more up-to-speed with current practice than I am.

As far as American English is concerned, apart from the ones listed above, verbs in British English that are traditionally spelled with *-ise* at the end are *always* spelled with *-ize* at the end in American English:

British	US
apologise	apologize
organise	organize
recognise	recognize

• Words ending in *-yse*

Verbs in British English that end in *-yse* are always spelled *-yze* in American English:

British	US
analyse	analyze
breathalyse	breathalyse
paralyse	paralyze

- ## Words ending in *-our*

British English words ending in *-our* usually end in *-or* in American English:

British	US
colour	color
humour	humor
neighbour	neighbor

- ## Nouns ending with *-ence*

Some nouns that end with *-ence* in British English are spelled *-ense* in American English:

British	US
licence	license
offence	offense
pretence	pretense

Note that it is *some* nouns, not all. 'Intelligence', 'independence', 'incompetence', and 'incontinence', for example, keep the *-ence* ending in American English. Why is 'defence' 'defense' in American English, when 'difference' is 'difference' on both sides of the pond? Nobody knows. You've just got to live with it.

- **Nouns ending with *-ogue***

    Some nouns that end with *-ogue* in British English can end with either *-og* or *-ogue* in American English. You take your pick.

British	US
analogue	analog *or* analogue
catalogue	catalog *or* catalogue
dialogue	dialog *or* dialogue

- **Words ending in a vowel plus the letter 'l'**

    In British spelling, verbs ending in a vowel plus the letter 'l' double the 'l' when adding endings that begin with a vowel. In American English, the 'l' is not doubled:[23]

British	US
travel	*travel*
travelled	traveled
travelling	traveling
traveller	traveler

[23] Curiously, when it comes to the word 'enthral', in British English it is spelled with one 'l', but in American English 'enthrall' has two. Enthralling, or what?

• Words spelled with double vowels

British English words that are spelled with the double vowels *ae* or *oe* are just spelled with an *e* in American English:[24]

British	US
leukaemia	leukemia
manoeuvre	maneuver
oestrogen	estrogen

Different Words

'When I first came to America,' the actress Penélope Cruz once confessed, 'I made a lot of mistakes, like going to the hair salon and asking for a blow job instead of a blow dry.'

If you are trying to communicate with Americans, it's best to do so on their terms — using their terms, which are sometimes fundamentally different from ours. When we speak of a 'Yank', for example, we mean anyone of American origin; when Americans speak of a 'Yank', they mean someone from the Northern states.

---

[24] That said, there are exceptions to this rule. In American English 'archaeology' is still usually spelled the English way. There's neither rhyme nor reason for it. You've just got to learn this stuff.

British English	American English
accommodation	accommodations
action replay	instant replay
aeroplane	airplane
agony aunt	advice columnist
aluminium	aluminum
aniseed	anise
anticlockwise	counterclockwise
articulated lorry	tractor-trailer
aubergine	eggplant
baking tray	cookie sheet
bank holiday	legal holiday
beetroot	beet(s)
biscuit	cookie; cracker
black economy	underground economy
blanket bath	sponge bath
block of flats	apartment building
boiler suit	coveralls
bonnet (*of a car*)	hood
boot (*of a car*)	trunk
bottom drawer	hope chest
bowls	lawn bowling
braces	suspenders
breakdown van	tow truck
bumbag	fanny pack
candyfloss	cotton candy
car park	parking lot
casualty	emergency room

catapult	slingshot
central reservation	median strip
chemist	drugstore
chips	French fries
cinema	movie theater; the movies
cling film	plastic wrap
cos (*lettuce*)	romaine
cot	crib
cotton bud	cotton swab
cotton wool	absorbent cotton
courgette	zucchini
court card	face card
crash barrier	guardrail
crisps	chips; potato chips
crotchet (*music*)	quarter note
current account	checking account
danger money	hazard pay
dialling tone	dial tone
diamanté	rhinestone
double cream	heavy cream
draughts (*game*)	checkers
drawing pin	thumbtack
dressing gown	robe; bathrobe
drink-driving	drunk driving
drinks cupboard	liquor cabinet
drinks party	cocktail party
driving licence	driver's license
dual carriageway	divided highway

dummy (*for a baby*)	pacifier
dust sheet	drop cloth
dustbin	garbage can
engaged (*of a phone*)	busy
estate car	station wagon
ex-directory	unlisted
first floor	second floor
fish finger	fish stick
fitted carpet	wall-to-wall carpeting
flannel	washcloth
flat	apartment
flick knife	switchblade
flyover	overpass
football	soccer
fringe (*hair*)	bangs
full stop (*punctuation*)	period
garden	yard; lawn
gear lever	gearshift
gearing (*finance*)	leverage
goods train	freight train
greaseproof paper	wax paper/waxed paper
green fingers	green thumb
grill (*noun*)	broiler
grill (*verb*)	broil
ground floor	first floor
hen night	bachelorette party
hire purchase	installment plan
hoarding	billboard

hob	stovetop
holdall	carryall
holiday	vacation
homely	homey
in hospital	in the hospital
hot flush	hot flash
hundreds and thousands	sprinkles (*for ice cream*)
indicator (*on a car*)	turn signal
inside leg	inseam
jelly babies	jelly beans
Joe Bloggs	Joe Blow
Joe Public	John Q. Public
jumble sale	rummage sale
jump lead	jumper cable
jumper	sweater
junior school	elementary school
kennel	doghouse
ladybird	ladybug
a lettuce	a head of lettuce
level crossing	grade crossing
lift	elevator
lollipop lady (or man)	crossing guard
lolly	lollipop
loose cover	slipcover
lorry	truck
loudhailer	bullhorn
low loader	flatbed truck
lucky dip	grab bag

luggage van	baggage car
maize	corn
mangetout	snow pea
market garden	truck farm
marshalling yard	railroad yard
maths	math
milometer	odometer
minim (*music*)	half note
mobile phone	cell phone
monkey tricks	monkeyshines
motorway	expressway; highway
mum/mummy	mom/mommy
nappy	diaper
newsreader	newscaster
noughts and crosses	tic-tac-toe
number plate	license plate
off-licence	liquor store; package store
oven glove	oven mitt
paddling pool	wading pool
paracetamol	acetaminophen
parting (*in hair*)	part
patience (*game*)	solitaire
pavement	sidewalk
pay packet	pay envelope
pedestrian crossing	crosswalk
pelmet	valance
petrol	gas; gasoline
physiotherapy	physical therapy
pinafore dress	jumper

plain chocolate	dark chocolate
plain flour	all-purpose flour
polo neck	turtleneck
positive discrimination	reverse discrimination
postal vote	absentee ballot
postbox	mailbox
postcode	zip code
power point	electrical outlet
pram	baby carriage; stroller
press-up	pushup
private soldier	GI
public school	private school
public transport	public transportation
punchbag	punching bag
pushchair	stroller
quantity surveyor	estimator
quaver (*music*)	eighth note
queue	line
racing car	race car
railway	railroad
recorded delivery	certified mail
registration plate	license plate
remould (*tyre*)	retread
reverse the charges	call collect
reversing lights	back-up lights
right-angled triangle	right triangle
ring road	beltway
roundabout (*at a fair*)	carousel

roundabout (*in a road*)	traffic circle
rowing boat	rowboat
sailing boat	sailboat
saloon (*car*)	sedan
sandpit	sandbox
sandwich cake	layer cake
sanitary towel	sanitary napkin
self-raising flour	self-rising flour
semibreve (*music*)	whole note
semitone (*music*)	half step
shopping trolley	shopping cart
silencer (*on a car*)	muffler
silverside	rump roast
skeleton in the cupboard	skeleton in the closet
skimmed milk	skim milk
skipping rope	jump rope
skirting board	baseboard
sledge	sled
sleeper	railroad tie
sleeping partner	silent partner
slowcoach	slowpoke
snakes and ladders	chutes and ladders
solicitor	lawyer
soya/soya bean	soy/soybean
splashback	backsplash
spring onion	scallion
stag night	bachelor party
Stanley knife	utility knife
starter	appetizer

state school	public school
storm in a teacup	tempest in a teapot
surtitle	supertitle
swede	rutabaga
sweets	candy
takeaway (*food*)	takeout; to go
taxi rank	taxi stand
tea towel	dish towel
terrace house	row house
tick	check mark
ticket tout	scalper
timber	lumber
titbit	tidbit
toffee apple	candy apple or caramel apple
touch wood	knock on wood
trade union	labor union
trading estate	industrial park
trainers	sneakers
trolley	shopping cart
underground	subway
vacuum flask	thermos bottle
verge (*of a road*)	shoulder
vest	undershirt
veterinary surgeon	veterinarian
wagon (*on a train*)	car
waistcoat	vest
walking frame	walker
wardrobe	closet
weatherboard	clapboard

white coffee	coffee with cream
wholemeal bread	wholewheat bread
windscreen	windshield
wing (*of a car*)	fender
worktop	countertop
zebra crossing	crosswalk
zed (*letter Z*)	zee
zip	zipper

Stiff Upper Lip

When it comes to American words and phrases creeping into British English, I like to think that I keep my cool and maintain my stiff upper lip. I'm that phlegmatic because I happen to know that 'keeping your cool' and 'stiff upper lip' are both American in origin. We may now think of the 'stiff upper lip' — showing fortitude in the face of adversity and self-restraint in place of quivering-upper-lip emotion — as a quintessentially British attribute, but the phrase originated in America in 1815 and became popular thanks to the success of a poem by the American women's rights activist Phoebe Cary (1824–71), which featured the lines, 'And though hard be the task, / "Keep a stiff upper lip".'

The reliable, talented, and influential British journalist Matthew Engel, author of the tremendous *That's the Way It Crumbles: The American Conquest of the English Language*, is the acknowledged authority on Americanisms that have successfully invaded British English. The list of them is lengthy — and, as Matthew points out, includes 'lengthy', as well as 'reliable', 'talented', 'influential', and 'tremendous': 'All of these words we use without a second thought were not normally part of the English language until the establishment of the United States. The Americans imported English wholesale, forged it to meet their own needs, then exported their own words back across the Atlantic to be incorporated in the way we speak over here. Those seemingly innocuous words caused fury at the time. The poet Coleridge denounced "talented" as a barbarous word in 1832, though a few years later it was being used by William Gladstone. A letter-writer to *The Times*, in 1857, described "reliable" as vile.'

Some modern American imports, Matthew can't stand – among them 'faze' (as in 'it doesn't faze me'), 'hospitalize', 'elevator', 'rookies' (for 'newcomers'), and 'guy': 'less and less the centrepiece of the ancient British festival of 5 November — or, as it will soon be known, 11/5. Now someone of either gender.' However, sometimes, he concedes, American phrases can have 'vigour and vivacity': 'A relative of mine told me recently he went to a business meeting chaired by a Californian woman who wanted everyone to speak frankly. It was "open kimono".'

When Matthew wrote about this for the BBC, the BBC invited the public to send in their own pet aversions (English), *bêtes noires* (French), and bugaboos (American). Here are just forty of the Americanisms it seems the public *really* can't stand.

1. When people ask for something, I often hear: **'Can I get a ...'** It infuriates me. It's not New

York. It's not the 90s. You're not in Central Perk with the rest of the Friends. Really.

2. The next time someone tells you something is the **'least worst option'**, tell them that their most best option is learning grammar.

3. The phrase I've watched seep into the language (especially with broadcasters) is **'two-time'** and **'three-time'**. Have the words double, triple, etc, been totally lost?

4. Using **24/7** rather than '24 hours, 7 days a week' or even just plain 'all day, every day'.

5. The one I can't stand is **'deplane'**, meaning to disembark an aircraft, used in the phrase 'you will be able to deplane momentarily'.

6. **'Touch base'** — it makes me cringe no end.

7. Is **'physicality'** a real word?

8. **Transportation**. What's wrong with transport?

9. Does nobody celebrate a birthday any more, must we all **'turn'** 12 or 21 or 40?

10. What kind of word is **'gotten'**? It makes me shudder.

11. **'I'm good'** for 'I'm well'. That'll do for a start.

12. **'Bangs'** for a fringe of the hair.

13. **Take-out** rather than takeaway!

14. **'A half hour'** instead of 'half an hour'.

15. A **'heads up'**. For example, as in a business meeting. Let's do a 'heads up' on this issue. I have never been sure of the meaning.

16. **Train station.** My teeth are on edge every time I hear it. Who started it? Have they been punished?

17. To put a list into alphabetical order is to **'alphabetise it'** — horrid!

18. People that say **'my bad'** after a mistake. I don't know how anything could be as annoying or lazy as that.

19. **'Normalcy'** instead of 'normality' really irritates me.

20. **Eaterie.** To use a prevalent phrase, oh my gaad!

21. I'm a Brit living in New York. The one that always gets me is the American need to use the word **bi-weekly** when fortnightly would suffice just fine.

22. I hate **'alternate'** for 'alternative'. I don't like this as they are two distinct words, both have distinct meanings and it's useful to have both. Using alternate for alternative deprives us of a word.

23. **'Hike'** a price. Does that mean people who do that are hikers? No, hikers are ramblers!

24. **Going forward?** If I do I shall collide with my keyboard.

25. The most annoying Americanism is **'a million and a half'** when it is clearly one and a half million! A million and a half is 1,000,000.5 where one and a half million is 1,500,000.

26. **'Reach out to'** when the correct word is 'ask'. For example: 'I will reach out to Kevin and let you know if that timing is convenient'. Reach out? Is Kevin stuck in quicksand? Is he teetering on the edge of a cliff? Can't we just ask him?

27. Surely the most irritating is: **'You do the Math.'** Math? It's MATHS.

28. I hate the fact I now have to order a **'regular Americano'.** What ever happened to a medium-sized coffee?

29. My worst horror is **expiration,** as in 'expiration date'. Whatever happened to expiry?

30. I am increasingly hearing the phrase **'that'll learn you'** – when the English (and more correct) version was always 'that'll teach you'. What a ridiculous phrase!

31. I really hate the phrase: **'Where's it at?'** This is not more efficient or informative than 'where is it?' It just sounds grotesque and is immensely irritating.

32. My pet hate is **'winningest',** used in the context 'Michael Schumacher is the winningest driver of all time'. I can feel the rage rising even using it here.

33. My brother now uses the term **'season'** for a TV series. Hideous.

34. Having an **'issue'** instead of a 'problem'.

35. I hear more and more people pronouncing the letter Z as **'zee'.** Not happy about it!

36. To '**medal**' instead of to win a medal. Sets my teeth on edge with a vengeance.

37. '**I got it for free**' is a pet hate. You got it 'free' not 'for free'. You don't get something cheap and say you got it 'for cheap' do you?

38. 'Turn that off **already**'. Oh dear.

39. '**I could care less**' instead of 'I couldn't care less' has to be the worst. Opposite meaning of what they're trying to say.

40. Dare I even mention the **fanny pack**?

The Americanised version of *Harry Potter and the Philosopher's Stone* refers to 'English muffins' instead of 'crumpets'. It has come to this.

7. A Bad Spell of Whether

Whether the weather be fine,
Whether the weather be not,
We must weather the weather
Whatever the weather,
Whether we like it or not.

'Whether' and 'weather' are homophones. They are heterographs, too.

Homophones are words that sound the same, but have different meanings. ('Homophone' derives from the Greek *homo-*, meaning 'same', and *phone*, meaning 'voice'.) **Heterographs** are words that sound the same, but are spelled differently and have different meanings. (*Hetero-* meaning 'different' in Greek; *graph* meaning 'writing'.) Here are a dozen more homophonic heterographs:

aural — oral
bald — bawled
band — banned
bard — barred
bear — bare
for — fore — four
here — hear
pare — pair — pear
raw — roar

there — their
toad — towed
to — too — two

Homographs are words that sound and are spelled the same, but have different meanings — *viz*:

bat — a piece of sporting equipment / a winged animal
down — in a lower position / soft feathers
evening — after the afternoon / making more even
incense — a substance that produces an odour when
burned / to infuriate and make angry
proceeds — continuing on / the money or profit
gained from a venture
second — 1/60th of a minute / after the first

Heterophones are words that are spelled the same, but are pronounced differently and have different meanings — *viz*:

bass — a type of fish / a low, deep voice
bow — a type of knot / to incline forward
entrance — the way in / to delight
does — a number of female deer / the third person
singular form of the verb 'to do'
tear — to rip / a drop of water from the eye
wind — moving air / turning

Heterophones can cause confusion. When Endeavour Morse comes across the text from the murder suspect that reads, 'My wife and I had a terrific row on Saturday,' does he think what took place was an unpleasant argument or a delightful boat trip along the River Isis?

Homophones are at the root of many a spelling error. Ignorance plays its part, too. When is it 'who's'? And when is it 'whose'? How do you choose? And what about words that sound similar, but aren't at all. Every two years: is that 'biennial' or 'biannual'? 'May I come in?' or 'Can I come in?' — is there a difference? Does it matter? There is and it does.

Two surveys — one of business emails, the other conducted by university lecturers asked to monitor the written work of first year students — have revealed the most common linguistic mistakes we make. And we do all make them — some, of course, more than others. To err is human. To arr is pirate… What a difference a single misplaced letter can make.

Here, then, is the Brandreth Guide to our worst word confusions and how to deal with them. These are the words and turns of phrase most people manage to mangle most often. In most instances, putting matters right is just a matter of being aware that they are wrong to start with. There is no substitute for simply learning (and remembering) what's right and what's wrong, but, to help, I have come up with some tips — my little secrets, acronyms, and observations — to point you in the right direction.

abuse / misuse / disabuse
abuse = maltreatment

misuse = incorrect treatment

disabuse = persuade that an idea or belief is mistaken

Secret: simply learn what each word means, remembering that there is an 'a' upfront in 'abuse' and 'maltreatment' and an 'i' upfront in 'misuse' and 'incorrect'.

accept / except

accept = consent to receive

except = not including, excluding

Secret: add '-ional' and see what happens — 'exceptional' makes sense; 'acceptional' doesn't.

acute / chronic (of an illness)

acute = an illness that is sudden and short-lived

chronic = an illness that persists for a long time

Secret: an 'a**cut**e illness' **cut**s right in; a chronic illness goes **on** and **on** and **on**.

affect / effect (nouns)

affect = in psychology, the emotion associated with an idea

effect = the result or consequence of an action

Secret: 'affect' as a noun is very rare, so don't worry about it; 'effect' is almost certainly the noun you need.

affect / effect (verbs)

to affect = to have an effect on; to make a difference to

To effect = to make something happen

Secret: to affect something you need to make **a** difference; to **effect** a change you need to be **effect**ive.

aggravate / annoy

aggravate = make worse

annoy = irritate

Secret: something that's aggravating is annoying; remember that 'grave' means 'serious' and 'bad' — to 'ag**grav**ate' is worse.

alternate / alternative

alternate (*adjective*) = every other
alternative = another possibility or choice, different
to alternate (*verb*) = to go from one to another
Secret: put the definitions into the sentence to see if they make sense.

among / between

among = situated more or less centrally in
relation to several other things
between = at, in, or across the space
separating two things
Secret: use 'between' for **two** things, 'among' for many.

amount / number

amount = a general quantity of something
number = a specific quantity
Secret: use 'amount' for what you cannot count – 'I like a generous amount of coffee in the cafetière; I'd say three spoonfuls in number.'

ante- / anti-

ante- = before
anti- = against
Secret: there is an '**e**' in **ante-** which means '**be**fore' (as in 'antecedents' and 'ante-natal'); there is an '**a**' in **anti-** which means '**a**gainst' (as in 'anti-depressant' and 'anti-apartheid').

as / like

Secret: **as** can be an adverb, a conjunction, or a preposition; ditto **like**, which can be an adjective, a noun, and a verb as

172

well. They are often interchangeable, but, as a rule, use **as** before phrases and clauses, and **like** before nouns and pronouns – *viz* 'I love you **as** I used to do' sounds better than 'I love you **like** I used to do'; and 'He looks **like** Donald Duck' is correct while 'He looks **as** Donald Duck' is incorrect; and 'He looks **like** Donald Duck did' is better than 'He looks **as** Donald Duck did'. Because **like** is now such an overused work, opt for **as** when you have a choice. In your head think back to Ernie Wise and the plays like what he wrote. If it sounds like Ernie speaking, avoid.

assume / deduce
assume = suppose to be the case, without proof
deduce = work out to be the case, from the facts
Secret: **as**suming is what you **s**uppose, **d**educing **d**epends on **d**ata.

bare / bear
bare = naked
bear = an animal, or to carry or tolerate
Secret: when you are **bar**e in the bath you use your **bar** of soap; b**ears** have **ears**; when you **bear** a burden you feel as strong a **bear**.

bated / baited
bated = in suspense
baited = something prepared (like bait)
to lure a creature
Secret: remember my cat, Oscar, who always ate cheese for supper so that he could sit by the mouse hole with baited bated breath.

biannual / biennial
biannual = twice a year
biennial = every two years

Secret: there are two 'a's in one **annual**; there is an 'e' in 'every two years'.

bored with / bored by / bored of

Secret: consider the alternatives — 'I'm bored **with** learning grammar'; 'I'm bored **by** learning grammar'; 'I'm bored **of** learning grammar'. Which one would you use? Either the first or the second, I bet. I'm sure you, like me, disapprove of 'bored **of**'. Unfortunately, the world is against us on this. I have consulted my friends at the Oxford University Press and this is their verdict: 'The first two constructions, bored with and bored by, are the standard ones. The third, bored of, is more recent than the other two and it's become extremely common. It represents a perfectly logical development of the language, and was probably formed on the pattern of expressions such as "tired of" or "weary of". Nevertheless, some people dislike it and it's not fully accepted in standard English. It's best to avoid using it in formal writing.' That's something.

capital / capitol

Secret: when the word 'Capitol' is capitalised, it refers to the United States Capitol building in Washington, DC, home of Congress, the legislative branch of the US federal government. Both **capital** and **capitol** are derived from the Latin root *caput*, meaning 'head', but the building that is a **capitol** often has a dome that looks

like an 'o' — and both dome and capitol have an 'o' —
while **A**lgiers is the capital of **A**lgeria and with a capital
like **A**nkara you are talking Turkey.

compared with / compared to

Secret: American English favours 'compared **to**' and
British English prefers 'compared **with**'. If in doubt use
'compared **with**'. Though some authorities say the two
are interchangeable, there is a difference between them.
'To compare **to**' is to highlight resemblances between
objects regarded as essentially of a different order — e.g.
'Shall I compare thee to a summer's day?' 'To compare
with' is to highlight differences between objects regarded
as essentially of the same order — e.g. 'This summer
compares favourably with last summer.'

complement / compliment

complement = something that contributes something
extra to something

compliment = a nice thing to say

Secret: **ee** lad, what compl**e**ments something compl**e**tes
something; aye, aye (**I, i**), a compl**i**ment is a form of
politeness – and compl**i**mentary drinks are fine liquids
to imbibe.

continual / continuous

continual = happening over and over again

continuous = non-stop

Secret: **continual** love-making is exhilarating; **continuous**
love-making is exhausting.

could have / could of

Secret: 'could **have**' is correct, 'could **of**' is wrong. People get it wrong because the phrases sound a bit alike. Just remember that 'could' must be followed by a four-letter word: 'have'.

defuse / diffuse

defuse = remove a fuse; make a situation less dangerous
diffuse = spread

Secret: with '**de**fuse', picture yourself taking out that fuse; **diff**use is **diff**erent.

desert / dessert

desert = a stretch of sand; to leave or abandon
dessert = a pudding

Secret: in the French Foreign Legion some deserted in the desert; the desert is arid, but de**ss**erts are **s**weet and **s**ugary and have a double '**s**' as **s**weets do.

different from / different to / different than

Secret: of the three, 'different **from**' is the most common and, in my view, the one to use. 'This book is different **from** all the others' just sounds better to my ears than 'This book is different **to** all the others' (which is acceptable) or 'This book is different **than** all the others' — which would be acceptable in American English but not in British English.

And while we're at it, what about 'similar **to**' versus 'similar **from**'? 'Similar **to**' is correct. If things differ, they differ away from each other. If they are similar, they are similar towards each other.

disaffected / unaffected
disaffected = dissatisfied
unaffected = not affected
Secret: it's '**d**' for '**d**issatisfaction' and '**n**' for **n**ot as in 'not affected'.

discreet / discrete
discreet = careful, prudent, unobtrusive, secret
discrete = separate and distinct
Secret: with 'discreet' there are 't's at the ends of the relevant words – prudent, secret, tact; with 'discrete' the 't' is there to keep the two 'e's separate and distinct.

disinterested / uninterested
disinterested = showing no partiality
uninterested = not interested
Secret: if you are **dis**interested, you keep your emotional **dis**tance because you are neutral.

draught / draft
draught = a current of cool air; a single gulp of a drink
draft = a rough version of something;
to recruit somebody
Secret: Americans spell both versions one way — 'draft'; but if yo**u** are British, remember yo**u** are as yo**u** feel the cold air c**u**rrent and you drink your dra**u**ght of p**u**re ale.

due to / owing to
due to = caused by
owing to = because of

Secret: there is a subtle difference between the phrases, but, happily, it's one we don't worry too much about any more. As a rule, **owing to** is more likely to be used at the start of a sentence and **due to** within a sentence; but **owing to** changes in the way we treat our language (some might say that's **due to** poor teaching), with 'owing to' and 'due to', you can do as you please.

elude / allude
elude = escape from, avoid
allude = make reference to
Secret: 'e' for 'elude' and 'e' for 'escape'; 'a' for 'allude', which brings attention with it.

ensure / insure
ensure = make certain
insure = take precautions against risk
Secret: 'e' is in 'certain'; 'i' is in 'risk'.

especially / specially
especially = particularly
specially = particularly
Secret: the two are almost interchangeable, although **especially** is used much more often than **specially**. **Especially** should be used to single something out — e.g. 'I love the Marx Brothers, especially Harpo' — and **specially** should be used to signify a **special** purpose — e.g. 'I wore the curly wig specially in his honour.'

fall pregnant / become pregnant

Secret: avoid 'falling pregnant' — at least, avoid using the phrase. It suggests either that the pregnancy was a chance accident (as in 'she fell over') or a biblical punishment (as in the Fall of Adam and Eve) and is generally considered outdated, if not offensive. When they debated the phrase on Mumsnet, most of the contributors did not approve: 'Upduffed is at least trying to be funny. Fell pregnant is all faux-naive whoopsiedaisy.' 'Drives me nuts too. Everytime I hear it.'

farther / further

farther = a physical distance away

further = a more figurative distance away

Secret: 'far**ther**' contains the word **far**; 'further' is used to relate to time and ideas, rather than specific distance — e.g. 'Further down the line he promised to come up with further plans'. But they are really interchangeable, and 'further' is now more often used than 'farther', so move farther down the page, please, and don't worry yourself with further thoughts on this.

flank / flanked

flank = one side

flanked = on both sides

Secret: you've just got to learn this. An animal's **flank** is its side, between the ribs and the hip. A **flank** of an army or navy force is one side of it when it is organised for battle. But if something **is flanked by** things, it has them on both sides of it.

179

fortuitous / fortunate

fortuitous = by chance

fortunate = good fortune

Secret: fortunately, 'fortunate' almost contains the word 'fortune'; 'fortuitous' contains a couple of 'u's for luck.

forward / foreword

forward = at the front and moving ahead

foreword = a short introduction to a book

Secret: to go forward with an 'a' means to advance; a foreword contains words that appear before the rest of the book.

hear / here

hear = what you do with your ears

here = the place where you are

Secret: the ear in 'hear' is the give-away.

historic / historical

historic = important in history

historical = to do with history

Secret: a historic event is significant; a historical event is anything that happened in the past.

a hotel / an hotel

Secret: many people believe they should use the indefinite article an instead of a and speak of 'an hotel' and 'an historic event'. They're wrong. We use an in front a spoken vowel sound, regardless of spelling, so it's 'an animal', 'an orange', and 'an idea'; and because the 'h' is silent it's '**an** heir', '**an** hour', and '**an** honour'. Where the '**h**' is pronounced we use an **a**, so it's '**a** house', '**a** hippopotamus', and '**a** hair'. In the eighteenth century, pronunciation was different and people pronounced 'hotel' 'otel'. Not any more, which is why '**a** hotel', '**a** historic event', and '**a** horrific happening' are correct today.

hopefully / hopefully
hopefully = in a hopeful way
hopefully = expressing what you hope will happen
Secret: once upon a time, **hopefully** simply meant 'full of hope', as in: 'He looked on life **hopefully**.' But increasingly the word is used, especially at the start of a sentence, to indicate a hope that something might happen, as in: **'Hopefully** I'll get to Heaven one day.'

hung / hanged
hung = the past and past participle of hang
hanged = what happens in death by hanging
Secret: once **hung** and **hanged** were interchangeable; not any more. Pictures, meat, and the well-endowed are all **hung**, but someone who has been executed by hanging is always said to have been **hanged**.

imply / infer
imply = to suggest or hint at
infer = to deduce or conclude
Secret: if you're a bit **imp**ish you might **imp**ly something naughty; with a **fer**ocious intellect you can in**fer** what's going on.

in / into, on / onto

in and on indicate place or location

into and onto indicate directions of motion

Secret: use **in** or **on** to refer to something in relation to a larger area around it — e.g. 'Liz is **in** the kitchen; Buzz is **on** the moon.' Use **into** or **onto** to indicate movement — e.g. 'Buzz climbed **into** the rocket; Liz jumped **onto** the table.' Some authorities suggest that 'in to' and 'on to' should each always be written as two words. Not so. It depends on the context — e.g. 'Liz walked **in to** the village and then, near-blind as she is, walked **into** the lamp post'; 'The spaceship fell **onto** the ground, though the hope had been that it would fly **on to** Jupiter'. **Into** can also be used to mean 'enthusiasm': 'He's **into** sado-masochism.' **On to** can also be used to mean 'awareness': 'She's **on to** him.'

in /on

in = inside or within

on = on top or above

Secret: I wrote a biography of the Duke of Edinburgh and said in it that, during the Second World War, Prince Philip had 'served on HMS *Ramillies*'. His Royal Highness corrected me: 'I did not serve on HMS *Ramillies*.' 'But you did, sir,' I protested. 'I have seen the logbook. You served on HMS *Ramillies*, no question.' The Duke looked at me witheringly: 'I did not serve **on** HMS *Ramillies*, I served **in** HMS *Ramillies*. You don't live **on** your house, do you? You live **in** your house.' I learned a useful lesson from the royal rebuke: you ride **on** a camel, you travel **in** a train; you ride **on** a bicycle, you fly **in** an aeroplane.

invite / invitation
'invite' is the verb
'invitation' is the noun

Secret: you **invite** someone to a party by sending them an **invitation**. At least, that's the way I do it, but 'invite' as a colloquial form of 'invitation' has being going the rounds since at least the mid-seventeenth century. **Invite**, with the accent on the second syllable, is the verb and there is no dispute about it. But **invite**, with the accent on the first syllable, is now used almost universally as a noun meaning **invitation**. I don't like it, but everybody else seems to.

lay / lie / laid

Secret: **lay** is a transitive verb, which means it requires one or more objects — as in: 'I lay the table; you lay down the law; she is the goose that lays the golden eggs.' **Lie** is an intransitive verb, which cannot have a direct object following it. (Many verbs can be both transitive and intransitive, but some, like 'lie', 'arrive', 'go', 'sneeze', 'sit', and 'die', for example, are always intransitive.) This, of course, is 'lying' in the sense of lying horizontal. So, today, in the present, you can **lie** in bed all day and the hen can **lay** the eggs; yesterday, in the past, you **lay** in bed all day and the hen **laid** her eggs. 'Lying' when it means 'telling lies' is a different word altogether and the past of this 'lie' is 'lied'. Men can rarely do two things at once, but the rogue husband managed it when he woke up in the dark and wondered who he was lying next to.[25]

---

[25] 'Getting laid', meaning 'having sex', is a phrase that seems to have originated in the US in the 1930s. No one is sure of its etymology.

lead / led

lead = the present tense of the verb 'to lead'

led = the past tense of the verb 'to lead'

Secret: the past tense of the verb **lead** is **led**, not **lead**. People get confused because the past tense of the verb **read** is not **red** but **read**. With **lead** and **led**, it's different: 'Let me **lead** you to the truth of the matter: she **led** me down the garden path.' The confusion is compounded by the fact that the metal **lead** (pronounced to rhyme with 'bed') is spelled the same way as the present tense of **lead** (pronounced to rhyme with 'bead') but sounds like **led**.[26]

lend / loan

Secret: **to lend** is the verb and **loan** is traditionally a noun, as in: 'I **lend** him some money; I give him a **loan**.' To keep the difference in mind, remember: in the **end** what you **lend** is a **loan**. That said, more and more people are using **loan** as a verb, but they're not necessarily people you should trust — e.g. 'The bank will **loan** you whatever you want if you can show them you don't need it.'

'Laid up', meaning 'being poorly', was originally a nautical term, dating from the late eighteenth century, describing a ship moored in harbour. 'Laid off', meaning 'made unemployed', dates from 1916; and 'laid-back', meaning 'relaxed', comes from the early 1970s and probably refers to the sitting stance of *Easy Rider*-style highway motorcyclists.

[26] Incidentally, the lead in your pencil almost certainly isn't. That's just what we call it. It's usually a form of graphite. And the LED written in capitals is the acronym for 'Light Emitting Diode'.

less / fewer

less = not as much

fewer = not as many

Secret: the **fewer** mistakes you make, the **less** you have to worry about. Use **fewer** when referring to people or things in the plural — e.g. 'Fewer men wax their chests in Lancashire than in any other English county'; 'the British smoke **fewer** cigarettes than the Italians'. Use **less** when referring to something that cannot be individually counted or does not have a plural, like 'love' or 'money' or 'time' or 'space' or 'music' or 'shopping' — e.g. 'There is **less** in-breeding in East Anglia than people suppose'; 'I listen to **less** music now my hearing's gone'. **Less** is also used with numbers when they are on their own and with expressions of measurement or time — e.g. 'Oxford is **less** than a hundred miles from Cambridge'; 'They were going out for **less** than two months'. Essentially, **fewer** is used to describe things that can be counted and **less** to describe things that can't — which is why, intriguingly, supermarket check-outs are correct when the signs they display read '5 items or **less**' because that refers to a total amount: '5 items or **fewer**' would place the emphasis incorrectly on each individual item.

licence / license

Secret: remember that **licence** is a noun and is what you get given when you pass your driving test and are then **licensed** to drive. **License** is both a noun and a verb in the United States, unlike every other English-speaking country. How to remember? The United **S**tates features two letter 's's: 'license'/'license'. English has only one: 'licence'/'license'. And in the UK, if you're a card-carrying licence-holder, you can think of the two 'c's in card-carrying and licence.

loose / lose

loose = to release something

lose = to be unable to find or keep something

Secret: **loose** rhymes with 'goose' and **lose** rhymes with 'snooze'. Picture a bow that you **loose** and you will see the double-**o**.

may / can

Secret: 'May I have the prawn cocktail, please?' 'Can I get the sashimi starter?' May I? Can I? Which is better? In fact, when the verbs **may** and **can** are used to ask for or grant permission, you **may** use either — yes, you really **can**. Because I belong to an older generation, and it is more courteous, I always use **may**. My children and grandchildren mostly use **can**. You also use **can**, of course, with questions of ability or capacity — e.g. '**Can** you dance?' '**Can** you call me on Friday?' — but that's a different question and does not affect the acceptability of using **can** when seeking or granting permission. That's the Brandreth Rule, but not everyone agrees with me. My friend, Bernard C. Lamb, distinguished President of the Queen's English Society, believes that 'May I?' is a request for permission while 'Can I?' asks whether I am able to do something — and has written a nifty limerick to illustrate the difference:

A lover of English named Ann
Asked: 'Please may I sleep with this man?'
When told: 'No, you can't!'
She replied: 'But, dear aunt,
Experience proves that I can.'

may / might

Secret: these days **may** and **might** are used interchangeably when referring to possibility and probability, but there is a difference between the two. **May** is used to express what is possible and real — e.g. 'He **may** die quite soon'; 'I **may** have muesli for breakfast'; 'They **may** get together'. **Might** is used to express what is hypothetical, less likely, or remotely possible — e.g. 'He **might** die, who knows?'; 'I **might** try muesli for a change'; 'They **might** get together, but I doubt it'. Remember **might** suggests a lower probability than **may**. '**Migh**ty unlikely' might be a useful mnemonic here.

maybe / may be

Secret: **maybe** is an adverb meaning 'perhaps'; **may be** is a combination of two verbs indicating possibility — e.g. '**Maybe** we'll go to the seaside today — there **may be** some sunshine.' To work out the difference in your head, substitute 'perhaps' for **maybe;** if it sounds right, **maybe** as one word is what you need.

maybe / perhaps
maybe = perhaps
perhaps = maybe

Secret: when I was a boy I was told to avoid **maybe** and always use **perhaps** instead. Times have changed and today the two words are almost interchangeable, though **perhaps** remains preferable in formal speech and writing.

mischievous / mischievious

Secret: **mischievous** (meaning 'full of mischief') is the correct way to spell **mischievous**. Adding that extra 'i' (and making the word rhyme with 'devious') is often done (and has been done for centuries) but it's wrong, wrong, wrong. Don't do it.

misremember / disremember

misremember = to remember incorrectly

disremember = to fail to remember, to forget

Secret: **disremember** is a wholly American word. If British English is what you speak, feel free to **disremember** it.

older / elder

older = elder

elder = older

Secret: **older** is the better word to use in most instances. **Elder** adds a level of respect that **older** does not — as in 'Respect your **elders**' and '**elder** statesmen' — but **elder** cannot be used when referring to objects or animals. 'She is my **elder** sister' is acceptable, but 'She is ten years **elder** than me' is not. As a rule, you'll be wiser to stick with **older**. (An **elder** is also a tree or shrub with white flowers and dark red berries, but that's another word altogether.)

188

oral / aural

oral = to do with the mouth

aural = to do with the ears

Secret: think of the 'o' in **oral** as the shape of the mouth and the '**au**' in **aural** as the same '**au**' in **au**dio and **au**ditory function and **au**dience. (Old joke alert. 'What's the worst thing about aural sex? The noise. What's the worst thing about oral sex? The view.')

orient / orientate

Secret: according to my copy of Fowler's *English Usage*: 'The shorter form [orient] emerged in the 18c. (first cited in Chambers Cyclopaedia of 1728) and the longer one [orientate], in the same sense (as in the French original), in the 19c. (1848), both with the meaning "to face or cause to face east" specifically in relation to the east–west alignment of churches. Both words then went in identical directions and developed the same extended senses: "to place in any particular way with respect to the cardinal points of the compass"; and, figuratively, "to ascertain one's 'bearings'."' Since they both have the same meaning, and **orient** is both more widely used and more concise than **orientate**, opt for **orient**.

over / more than

Secret: traditionalists believe that with countable numerical expressions you should use **more than** rather than **over**, **older than** rather than **over**, and **younger than** rather than **under** — so that 'It's **more than** 5,000 miles to San José' is correct, but 'It's **over** 5,000 miles to San José' is not, and 'She's **more than** forty, surely?' is right, but 'She's **over** forty, surely?' is wrong. But times change, and at the American Copy Editors Society annual gathering in 2014, two editors from the *Associated Press Stylebook*, the acknowledged grammar bible, declared that '**more than** and **over** are both acceptable in all uses to indicate a greater numerical value'. Some diehards protested — '**More than** my dead body!' read one outraged tweet — but generally, on both sides of the continent, it was agreed: the **more than** versus **over** conflict is at an end. The Brandreth Rule is: you can use them interchangeably when either makes sense, but essentially use **more than** with quantities and **over** with spatial relationships — e.g. 'Get it right and you'll be **over** the moon. Getting to the moon in the first place is the challenge. It's **more than** 238,000 miles away.'

passed / past

***Secret*: passed** is the past tense of the verb 'to pass' — as in: 'I **passed** my exam at the retake'; 'I **passed** Rumpelstiltskin on the stairs'. **Past** is not a verb, but a noun ('I'm living in the **past**'), an adjective ('the **past** tense'), an adverb ('the cat ran **past** me just now'), and a preposition ('Tea will be served at half **past** three'). The simplest way to work out if you should be using **past** or **passed** is to try writing what you want to say in the present tense. 'I **pass** my exam' works; 'Tea will be served at half **pass** three' doesn't.

peek / peep

peek = to look briefly while trying to avoid being seen

peep = to look through something, usually a hole

***Secret*:** you have a **peephole**, but never a **peekhole**.

pore/pour

pore = to study closely

pour = to flow or let flow

Secret: to pore — probably deriving from the verb 'to peer' — is used with either 'over' or 'through' and means 'to be absorbed in studying something closely', while 'to pour' means 'to flow or cause to flow in a steady stream'. When you po**re** over a book you are **re**ading, so **re**member the word ends in **re**. When you pour something it's often liquid — which could po**u**r from a ewer and the ewer-word is always spelt with a **u**.

practice / practise

Secret: in British English the **-ce** at the end of **practice** denotes the noun and the **-se** at the end of **practise** denotes the verb — as in 'advice' (noun) and 'advise' (verb) and 'device' (noun) and 'devise' (verb). It's easy to tell the difference with 'advice'/'advise' and 'device'/'devise' because the pronunciation is different, with '-ice' rhyming with 'ice' and '-ise' rhyming with 'eyes'. With **practice/ practise**, the pronunciation is the same, but think of 'advice'/'advise' and 'device'/'devise' and you've cracked the difference.

prescribe / proscribe

prescribe = to state authoritatively, to give authority for a medicine

proscribe = to forbid

Secret: you need a **prescri**ption in an **e**mergency, so it's an 'e' you're after; to **pro**scribe is to f**o**rbid, to rule **o**ut, so look out for the 'o'.

principal / principle

principal = chief, leading, main, most important

principle = a rule, a belief

Secret: keep the **Principal** on side, make her your **pal**; you can rely on her because she is a woman of **principle**.

program / programme

Secret: in British English a **programme** is a schedule of events, or a TV show, or what you get given at the theatre. In American English all those are simply **programs**. In British English a **program** is what you give to your computer.

rob / steal

rob = to take something without permission

steal = to take something without permission

Secret: but there is a difference. With **rob**, the emphasis is on the person or place from which the object is taken — e.g. 'The old lady was **robbed** of her savings'; 'It was her old man who **robbed** the bank'. With **steal**, the emphasis is on what's taken: 'She **stole** my watch and, later, my heart.' You **steal** an object, rather than **rob** it; you **rob** a place — unless it's a house, when you **burgle** it.

shopfitting / shoplifting

shopfitting = fitting out a shop

shoplifting = stealing from a shop

Secret: you know what they are and you know the difference between them. I've just popped them in here for fun because I came across a survey that showed that most people (55 per cent) when they see the word **shopfitting** initially read it as **shoplifting**.

sight / site / cite
sight = what you see
site = a place
cite = to quote

Secret: to help you with the different spellings involved here, remember that **sight** is all about seeing and **sight** requires l**ight**. A **site** (noun) is a place and **to site** (verb) is to place, so it's all about where things are **sit**uated. To **cite** means 'to quote', as in '**cit**ation'.

stationary / stationery
stationary = not moving
stationery = writing materials and the like

Secret: what's **stationary** is **static** with the emphasis on 'a'. **Stationery** (which you buy from a **stationer**) involves l**e**tters and **e**ndless **e**nvelopes with the emphasis on the 'e'.

there / their / they're
there = indicating a place
their = belonging to them
they're = they are

Secret: they all sound alike, but they are quite different. **There** indicates a place. **W**here? **H**ere? The letters 'here' are always **there** in '**there**'. **Their** means 'belonging to them' and the **heir**s hope to get what belongs to them. **They're** is simply a contraction of **they are**, so if in doubt say **they are** instead of **they're** and if it sounds right, it is. (The same goes when you want to tell the difference between **you're** and **your**.)

weather / whether / wether

weather = climate

whether = expressing a choice

wether = a sheep, usually a castrated ram

Secret: the **weather** can involve **heat**, **air**, and **atmosphere** and they all feature the letter 'a'. **Whether** or not the weather is fine is neither here nor there, with the emphasis on the letter 'e'. And with **wether**, the unfortunate castrated ram, there are a couple of things missing: the 'a' from **weather** and the 'h' from **whether**. (The 'bellwether', incidentally, is the leading sheep of the flock and wears a bell — hence the term 'bellwether', meaning 'something that leads or suggests a trend'.)

which / that / who

Secret: remember **who** and sometimes **that** refer to people, **that** and **which** refer to groups or things — e.g. 'I am the one **who** wrote this book, but you could say, "I am the one **that** wrote it." It is the book of **which** I am proudest — yes, the book **that** I'm most proud of.' **That** introduces what is called a 'restrictive clause', adding information that is vital to the point of the sentence — e.g. 'I like a book **that** has an arresting cover because it will sell more copies.' It's the phrase 'that has an arresting cover' that explains what type of book will sell more copies. **Which** introduces what is called a 'non-restrictive clause', adding non-essential supplementary information — e.g. 'The book, **which** has a great cover, is selling like hot cakes.' Restrictive clauses do not have commas introducing or surrounding them, whereas non-restrictive clauses do. Essentially, use **who** for humans and **which** for everything else, but note that

194

in times gone by the rule was looser — which is why the Lord's Prayer in the Book of Common Prayer begins 'Our Father **which** art in heaven', but in the 1928 Revised Prayer Book you find 'Our Father, **who** art in heaven'.

who's / whose

who's = who is

whose = belonging to

***Secret*: whose** is the possessive form of 'who' and **who's** is a contraction of 'who is' or 'who has' — e.g. '**Who's** going to tell me **whose** *Who's Who* that is?' To work out which you need, simply put 'who is' or 'who has' in your sentence and if it makes sense **who's** is what you're after — e.g. 'Who is line is it, anyway?' makes no sense, but '**Whose** line is it, anyway?' does.

who / whom

***Secret*:** 'Never send to know for **whom** the bells tolls; it tolls for thee.' The poet John Donne coined the phrase centuries before Ernest Hemingway wrote his novel and the Bee Gees and Metallica wrote their songs. Truth to tell, the bell may be tolling for **whom** soon. In a nutshell, **whom** is used in place of 'who' as the object of a verb or preposition — e.g. 'To **whom** am I speaking? **Whom** should I believe? With **whom** should I take a stroll?' Understanding when and how to use **whom** is not easy. Getting the use of **whom** wrong is easy. I could write a book about it — if you are interested you will find tens of thousands of words on the subject online — but I am not going to because I reckon the days of **whom** are numbered and somebody has already done it. Emmy

J. Favilla, the BuzzFeed Copy Chief, has written a book called *A World Without 'Whom'* and in it she issues her unequivocal rallying cry, 'Avoid **whom** altogether, for as long as you shall live!' She quotes Lisa McLendon, an editor and resident grammar expert at the University of Kansas, who told a roomful of copy editors: 'When in doubt, use **who** so you're not wrong *and* pretentious.' **Who** serves the purpose well enough — except where the word is preceded by what are known as 'quantifiers' such as 'all of', 'several of', 'some of', etc. — e.g. 'I know many English grammarians, most of whom are as dull as ditchwater.'

8. LOL — YOLO — Hahaha

How come the word 'abbreviation' is so long?

I don't know the answer to that. I do know that it originates with the Latin word for 'short' — *brevis*. I know, too, that we take all sorts of abbreviations for granted — like 'bus' for 'omnibus', 'gym' for 'gymnasium', 'exam' for 'examination', and 'pram' for 'perambulator'. I also know that it's a challenge these days to tell the difference between abbreviations, initialisms, and acronyms — the world is awash with the lot of them. WTF, eh?

Abbreviations are shorter spellings of words and expressions we use every day — like abbrev., Mr, Mrs, Ms, and St (for 'saint' or 'street'), etc. — and they are usually formed using the most noticeable letters from the word or expression. **Initialisms** are abbreviations, too, but in the form of the initial letters of the words they represent: RSVP for *'Répondez s'il vous plaît'* (French for 'Reply if you please'), 'm.p.h.' ('miles per hour'), BBC (British Broadcasting Corporation). **Acronyms** (from the Greek *acro*, here meaning 'point' or 'tip', and *nym* meaning 'name' or 'word') are abbreviations formed from the initial letters of other words and pronounced as a word — like 'radar' ('Radio Detection and Ranging') and AWOL ('Absent Without Leave').

When spoken out loud, most abbreviations are pronounced like the original word — 'Mr' is 'Mister' and 'etc.' is 'etcetera', etc. — but not always. For example, 'a.m.', 'p.m.', 'e.g.', and 'PhD' are abbreviations that are pronounced as they are spelled. 'Min.' and 'sec.' are pronounced 'minute' and 'second', but 'oz' and 'lb' are pronounced 'ounce' and 'pound' because they come from the Latin *uncia* and *libra*. Acronyms are pronounced as words when they can be — so POTUS and FLOTUS, for 'President of the United States' and 'First Lady of the United States', are pronounced 'potus' and 'flotus' — but not when they can't.[27] A BLT may be a 'bacon, lettuce, and tomato sandwich' but you call it a 'B, L, T'. A BLT will always be written in capitals, as will an ATM (Automated Teller Machine), but where the acronym is said as a word rather than as individual letters, you have a choice: it can be 'AWOL' or 'Awol', for example. With the acronym for 'Not in My Back Yard', it can be 'NIMBY' or 'Nimby', or even 'nimby', because the acronym has developed a life of its own thanks to the proliferation of 'nimbyism'.

Do you have to use a full stop at the end of an abbreviation? Sometimes, yes. Sometimes, no. Sometimes adding the full stop looks ugly and unnecessary — e.g. 'Capt. Reg. Smith, D.S.O.' At other times it may be helpful. For instance, 'a.m.' without punctuation can be confused with 'am'; 'pop.' is the abbreviation for 'population', but 'pop' without a full stop means several other things besides. Initialisms don't carry full stops these days (it's 'USA' not 'U.S.A.'; it's 'ATM' not 'A.T.M.'), nor do acronyms.

---

[27] POTUS does have a ring to it. In 2017, in the aftermath of President Donald Trump's introduction of a US travel ban affecting people from certain countries, a protestor appeared with a placard reading: 'Super callous fragile racist sexist Nazi POTUS'.

Sometimes it's helpful to explain an abbreviation or acronym the first time you use it, because not everyone may know what you mean — e.g. 'It was in 1999 that he first joined the RSC (Royal Shakespeare Company[28]) ...' Sometimes explaining the acronym doesn't help, because the acronym on its own tells the story — e.g. talking about your DNA or the AIDS epidemic makes more sense than talking about 'deoxyribonucleic acid' or 'Acquired Immune Deficiency Syndrome'. With GIF, few people seem to know it stands for 'Graphics Interchange Format', and, while in the US they often write it as 'GIF', in the UK it's mostly seen as 'gif', which helps differentiate it totally from TGIF, which is always written as 'TGIF' and stands for 'Thank God It's Friday'.

Acronyms are far from new — in the New Testament, for example, 'INRI' stands for 'Jesus of Nazareth King of the Jews' — but the use of them has exploded since the Second World War, which introduced hundreds to the language, from 'ack-ack' ('anti-aircraft') to 'jeep' (derived from 'GP' for 'General Purpose'[29]). I entered the world of acronyms big-time in the 1990s when I became an MP (Member of Parliament)

---

[28] Incredibly, some people believe that Francis Bacon actually wrote Shakespeare. It's unlikely, in my view. Besides, what self-respecting actor would want to join the Royal Bacon Company?

[29] 'General Purpose' was a phrase that gained currency during WWII (World War Two), but it is not established that the vehicle, the jeep, got its name that way. The first jeeps (which were specialised and not general purpose vehicles) were made by Ford and carried the initials 'GP', the 'G' being for 'government contract' and the 'P' as a code for a vehicle with an eighty-inch wheelbase. Later, servicemen using jeeps began to say the acronym stood for 'Just Enough Essential Parts'.

and PPS (Parliamentary Private Secretary), aspiring to be a PUSS (Parliamentary Under-Secretary of State). I was involved in politics and gender politics, for a while chairing a group known as LACVEE, pronounced 'Lacvee' and standing for 'Lesbians for a Conservative Victory'. I think some of the group had wanted Virginia Bottomley to head it up, but I was chosen instead. As my wife remarked at the time, 'Gyles, you're a lesbian's idea of a real man.'

One of my sisters was gay and a proper pioneer: in the 1970s she was part of a South London group known as TTLI — which stood for 'Tooting Lesbians Ignite'. But in the minefield of CSP — 'Contemporary Sexual Politics' — acronyms are up against a challenge as what began as the LGBT movement corners the market in available letters of the alphabet. At the time of going to press, the movement's full acronym runs to sixteen letters: LGBTQIACPGNCG-FNB, standing, proudly, for 'Lesbian, Gay, Bisexual, Transgender, Queer, Intersex, Asexual, Curious, Pansexual, Gender-non-conforming, Gender-fluid, Non-binary'.

By the way, that's not the world's longest acronym by any means. According to the *Guinness Book of World Records* the longest-ever acronym originated in the Soviet Union and ran to 56 letters (or 54 using the Cyrillic alphabet):

NIIOMTPLABOPARMBETZHELBETRABS-
BOMONIMONKONOTDTEKHSTROMONT

Apparently that stood for: 'The laboratory for shuttering, reinforcement, concrete, and ferroconcrete operations for composite-monolithic and monolithic constructions of the Department of the Technology of Building-assembly operations of the Scientific Research Institute of the Organisation for building mechanisation and technical aid of the Academy of Building and Architecture of the USSR'. The longest English acronym in current use is ADCOM-SUBORDCOMPHIBSPAC, used by the US Navy and standing for 'Administrative Command, Amphibious Forces, Pacific Fleet Subordinate Command'.

Back to the gender agenda, where an increasing number of people in the UK are identifying as MGB — or 'Mid-gender British'. (This could be confusing to an older generation who fondly remember the MGB roadster as a small car, albeit one with plenty of va-va-voom.) Apparently a lot of younger people now are ETS — which stands for 'Exploring the Spectrum' — which I like because it suggests an enquiring mind and a spirit of adventure. But if you know where you are and want an acronym to express yourself concisely, you can opt for SSS — which stands for 'Straight, Straight, Straight'.

SAH-WI is another acronym that's gaining currency — 'Straight and Happy With It' — though it sounds a bit defensive to me. Are the SAH-WI crowd protesting too much? 'SS' I quite like ('Simply Straight'), but I reckon SS-BOOP is a bit more likely to gain traction in the current climate. That's 'Simply Straight But Open to Other Possibilities'.

What am I? In principle I'm an HMMWTC: a 'happily married man with three children'. Okay, I invented that one, but there's no harm in being just that: a happily married man with three children. Look at Prince William. He's exactly that and seems to have decided where he is on the spectrum. Perhaps when you're already HRH KG KT PC ADC, you don't need to be LGBTQIA as well.

The use of acronyms has proliferated since the advent of the email in the 1970s and the start of text-messaging in the 1990s. With the arrival of Twitter in 2006 and the growth of every kind of social media platform since, new abbreviations and acronyms appear every day. That said, one of the ones we see most often dates back almost two hundred years to the invention of the typewriter and carbon paper at the beginning of the nineteenth century. When you send an email, you are invited to complete the top three lines — *viz*:

To:
Cc:
Bcc:

Here, the 'cc' stands for 'carbon copy'. In the days of the typewriter, two pieces of (usually) white typing paper were inserted into the machine with a piece of coloured carbon paper in between. What was typed on to the top piece of white paper appeared on the bottom piece of white paper thanks to the coloured carbon paper in between. The 'cc' on your email is the modern equivalent of the carbon copy — destined to be sent to whoever you choose. 'Bcc' stands for 'blind carbon copy' and is sent as a copy without the principal recipient having sight of who it's going to.[30]

---

[30] **Cc**, btw, is nothing to do with **cf**, though they are sometimes confused. **Cf** does not stand for 'copy follows', but is an abbreviation of the Latin *confer* or *conferatur*, meaning 'compare', and is used to refer the reader to other material in order to make a comparison with the topic being discussed: e.g. 'cf fns 1 & 2 on Latin abbreviations'. (**Fn** is the abbreviation for 'footnote'.)

Just as, in my experience, it is only older people (in their eighties and above) who still telephone you on the land line, I suspect it will be a very few of my older readers who are unfamiliar with the use of language on the internet. In emails and text correspondence now, shorthand is commonplace — *viz*:

2	4	B	C	I	O	R	U	Y
to / too	for	be	see	eye	owe	are	you	why

And acronyms are everywhere. These are among the most common and useful:

2FFU = Too Fast for You
4YEO = For Your Eyes Only
AFAIR = As Far as I Remember
AFK = Away from Keyboard
B2K = Back to Keyboard
DGMW = Don't Get Me Wrong
EOD = End of Discussion
FKA = Formerly Known As
FWIW = For What It's Worth
IMHO = In My Humble Opinion
IMNSHO = In My Not So Humble Opinion
LOL = Laughing Out Loud
MMW = Mark My Words
NOYB = None of Your Business
OMG = Oh My God
OT = Off Topic
OTOH = On the Other Hand
POV = Point of View

ROTFL = Rolling on the Floor Laughing
SCNR = Sorry, Could Not Resist
SFLR = Sorry for Late Reply
SPOC = Single Point of Contact
THX = Thanks
TYVM = Thank You Very Much
WFM = Works for Me
WTF = What the Fuck
YMMD = You Made My Day
YAM = Yet Another Meeting

Most of you, I know, will have known most of the above. If you are not so young, you may not be so familiar with some of the following, the favoured acronyms of the Snapchat and WhatsApp generations:

2moro	Tomorrow
2nte	Tonight
ASL	Age / Sex / Location?
B3	Blah, Blah, Blah
B4YKI	Before You Know It
BFF	Best Friends Forever
BM&Y	Between Me and You
BRB	Be Right Back
BRT	Be Right There
C-P	Sleepy
CTN	Cannot Talk Now
CUS	See You Soon
CWOT	Complete Waste of Time

CYT	See You Tomorrow
E123	Easy as 1, 2, 3
EM?	Excuse Me?
F2F	Face to Face
FC	Fingers Crossed
FOAF	Friend of a Friend
HAK	Hugs and Kisses
IDC	I Don't Care
IDK	I Don't Know
ILU / ILY	I Love You
IMU	I Miss You
IRL	In Real Life
J/K	Just Kidding
JC	Just Checking
JTLYK	Just to Let You Know
KFY	Kiss for You
KMN	Kill Me Now
KPC	Keeping Parents Clueless
L8R	Later
MoF	Male or Female
MTFBWY	May the Force Be with You
MYOB	Mind Your Own Business
NP	No Problem
NTIM	Not That It Matters
NVM	Never Mind
OATUS	On a Totally Unrelated Subject
OIC	Oh, I See
OMW	On My Way
OTP	On the Phone
PAL	Parents Are Listening
PAW	Parents Are Watching
PIR	Parent in Room
POS	Parent over Shoulder

PROP(S)	Proper Respect
RN	Right Now
RU	Are You
SEP	Someone Else's Problem
SITD	Still in the Dark
SLAP	Sounds Like a Plan
SMIM	Send Me an Instant Message
SO	Significant Other
TMI	Too Much Information
UR	Your / You Are
W8	Wait
WB	Welcome Back
WYCM	Will You Call Me?
WYWH	Wish You Were Here
XOXOXOX	Hugs, Kisses ...

So much for the acronyms favoured by Millennials and Generation Z.[31] My friend, Ken Thomson (a Baby Boomer

[31] Pronounced 'Generation Zee'. This is the 'now' generation, born in the internet age, and following on from the 'Millennials' (also known as 'Generation Y'), born in the 1990s. They were preceded by 'Generation X' (also known as 'Gen X'), born between the 1960s and 1980s, successors to the post-war 'Baby Boomers', who followed on from the so-called 'Silent Generation', born between the mid-1920s and mid-1940s, the cohort that followed the 'WWII Generation', better known in the US as the 'GI Generation' or 'the Greatest Generation', and in Australia as 'the Federation Generation', who grew up to fight in the Second World War and succeeded 'the Lost Generation', the ones who came of age during the First World War. The term 'Lost Generation' was coined by the American writer Gertrude Stein, and popularised by Ernest Hemingway, who used it as an epigraph for his novel *The Sun Also Rises* in 1926. No one is exactly sure where the names of the other

like me), sent me this helpful 'Texting Guide for Seniors' designed to assist both Baby Boomers and anyone from earlier generations who are happily still with us:

ATD = At the Doctor's
BFF = Best Friend Fell
BTW = Bring the Wheelchair
BYOT = Bring Your Own Teeth
FWIW = Forgot Where I Was
GGPBL = Gotta Go, Pacemaker Battery Low
GHA = Got Heartburn Again
IMHO = Is My Hearing-aid On?
LMDO = Laughed My Dentures Out
OMSG = Oh My! Sorry, Gas
ROFLACGU = Rolling on Floor Laughing
and Can't Get Up
TTYL = Talk to You Louder

It's not easy to keep pace with the ever-evolving acronym vocabulary of the social media age. It's a far cry from the language of Shakespeare, Milton, and Jane Austen, but it has its own energy, originality, and style, and, oddly, while a misplaced apostrophe drives me nuts, I have a soft spot for the bizarre internet neologisms of our time. I have made a note of some of my favourites, used both in online exchanges and IRL verbal jousting. If you are a Baby Boomer or one of the Silent Generation who's decided it's time to make a noise, read, mark, and learn. If you belong

---

'generations' spring from or what 'generation' is due to succeed 'Generation Z'.

to Generation Z and have other gems you'd like to share, do get in touch. As you know, I'm on Twitter @GylesB1.

AMA: Ask Me Anything

What It Means: what it says. I'm ready, waiting, and willing.

Bae: Babe / Before anyone else

What It Means: either as an abbreviation of 'babe' or as an acronym for 'Before Anyone Else', **bae** (pronounced 'bay') has been around for at least fifteen years as a term of endearment with particular reference to your boy-friend/girlfriend/significant other. In July 2014, with Pharrell Williams's song, 'Come Get It Bae', **bae** went global.

BFN: Big Fat Negative

What It Means: **BFN** used to stand for 'Bye for Now' and probably still does among the over-sixties. **BFN** can also stand for 'But Fuck Nothing', as in: 'Jeez — you know **BFN**!' But these days **BFN** appears most fre-quently in online exchanges between women in relation to pregnancy tests and stands for the result when it's a 'Big Fat Negative'. **BFP** stands for 'Big Fat Positive', of course, but does not appear to be so popular. Other acro-nyms that feature frequently on Mumsnet and in parenting manuals include **TTC** for 'Trying to Conceive'; and, after **H9**, standing for a 'happy and healthy nine months', comes **CIO** which means letting your baby 'Cry It Out'. **HPT** is a 'Home Pregnancy Test', **OPK** is an 'Ovulation Predic-tor Kit', **DPO** is 'Days Past Ovulation', **m/c** is a 'miscarriage', **m/s** is 'morning sickness'.

DAE: Does Anyone Else?

What It Means: in Korean, **dae** means 'the essence of cool' — as in: 'That's some haircut, Mr Kim! Dae!' In Scottish **dae** means 'do' — as in 'Dae ye ken John Peel?' Online **DAE** (in capitals), meaning 'Does Anyone Else ...', is generally a prefix to a question — as in: '**DAE** fancy a pint after work?'

Dafuq: What the fuck?

What It Means: **WTF** is *passé*, *déclassé*, and in every sense yesterday's acronym. Its contemporary equivalent is **dafuq**, an interjection typically used in response to something that makes no sense. 'You've gone vegan? **dafuq**.' It is correctly written without capital letters, spaces, or punctuation. (While here, I should mention **AF**, which stands for 'As Fuck', and, according to BuzzFeed Copy Chief, Emmy J. Favilla, 'just by the simple act of abbreviation, imparts a more fun, softened tone than the full phrase, much like how *F you* is so much cuter than a hearty *Fuck you*'.)

ELI5: Explain Like I'm 5

What It Means: neither a postcode nor a boy band, **ELI5** is what you say when someone has tried to tell you about the beauty of the clausal subjunctive.

FML: Fuck My Life

What It Means: this is an acronym you tag on to the end of an account of some unfortunate event in your life: 'The first three buses were full and the fourth, the one I got, broke down on Hammersmith Bridge. **FML**.' The acronym has spawned an FMyLife blog that serves as 'a recollection of everyday anecdotes likely to happen to anyone'. Posts on the site are short, user-submitted stories of unhappy happenings that begin with the word 'Today. . .' and end with **FML**. FMyLife receives more than 1.7 million hits each day. Here's the first story I hit on when I visited just now:

> Today, after 38 years of never meeting my dad, and paying a private investigator thousands of pounds over several weeks of searching, I found him living 2 floors down in the same block of flats. He's the grouchy downstairs neighbour I've hated for 6 years. FML

FTFY: Fixed That for You
What It Means: FTFY works at two levels. The first is literal: someone makes a mistake in what they've said or written and you correct it for them, adding **FTFY** as your pay-off: 'No you haven't just *laid* the au pair. You've just *paid* her. **FTFY**.' The second is sarcastic: 'Sent your wife a text saying you'd just laid the au pair. **FTFY**.'

Facepalm: 'Ugh, idiot.'
What It Means: if you're a character in a US sitcom, when someone does something stupid your palm hits your forehead. The word **facepalm** does the acting for you, conveying despairing amazement, disbelief, or disapproval. The heightened version of **facepalm** is **headdesk**, which is the word you use to express the frustration and dismay that's enough to make you bang your head against your desk. A milder version of both of these is **SMH**, which simply stands for 'Shaking My Head'. Picture it.

IRL: In Real Life

What It Means: 'the definition of "irony"? Telling someone on Facebook to get a life.' It's an old joke, but relevant
here, where **IRL** does not relate to the Republic of Ireland, but is used to differentiate between the virtual life
you lead online and what happens 'In Real Life'. It can be
used, too, to differentiate actors from the characters they
play: 'She's incredible as the Queen. And I hear she's
pretty regal **IRL**.'

JSYK: Just So You Know

What It Means: in the early days of the internet we used
to say **FYI** to add a sarcastic touch when conveying news
or putting someone right. Now we say **JSYK**. Searching
the internet just now for a real-life example of the acronym in action, this is the first one I came across:

Hey dude jsyk, I banged your girl last night

Lulz

What It Means: lulz is a corrupt descendant of **LOLs** —
the originals being 'Lots of Laughs' and 'Laugh Out Loud'
(not to be confused with the lower case **lol**, which stands for
'lots of love') — but no one is using **LOL** any more. It's in
the discarded pile with **WTF** and **FYI**. **Lulz** denotes something done for kicks, fun, excitement, laughs. You might
respond to the message '*Hey dude jsyk, I banged your girl last
night*' with the perfectly reasonable enquiry: 'Why?' Given
the state of the world, the answer to that might well be:

*For the **lulz***

QFT: Quoted for Truth

What It Means: **QFT** is another one that works at two levels. First, you use it as an indicator that you passionately agree with what's been said. Tom: 'Jeremy Corbyn is one of the great figures of our time.' Dick: '**QFT**.' Second, when someone says something that you reckon needs to be kept on record. Harry: 'Corbyn will never become prime minister.' Tom: '**QFT**.' **QFT** also stands for 'Quantum Field Theory', the theory of quantum mechanics applied to fields (oh yes), and for 'Quite Fucking True', and 'Quit Fucking Talking'. Context is everything. And tapping the right keys is pretty important, too. In the old days, when **WTF** was being tapped out on keyboards across the western world some did it at such speed that inadvertently they hit the 'Q' key when they meant to hit the 'W', which is how **QTF** gained currency. That's now the acronym for 'Que the Fuck', in which the Spanish *qué* replaces the English *what. Olé!*

Schrodinger's Douchebag

What it means: **Schrodinger's Douchebag** refers to someone who tests what they say before taking responsibility for what they've said. It's a very useful term for someone who makes **douchebag** (i.e. doubtful, inept, obnoxious) pronouncements, especially of a sexist, racist, or otherwise unacceptable and bigoted nature and then decides whether they were 'just joking' or meant it, depending on how others respond. The website urbandictionary.com gives this illustration of the phrase in action:

'Oh man, women should just stay in the kitchen,
it's the only place they're useful.'
with one group: 'Haha just kidding, that's sexist.'
with another: 'lol amirite.'
'You're a total schrodinger's douchebag, you know
that, right?'

TIL: Today I Learned

What It Means: when you discover something that isn't
new to the world but is new to you, you tag it with **TIL**.
'The word "geek" comes from a German word, *geck*,
meaning "fool, freak, or simpleton", and has been around
for centuries. Some people think the word "nerd" comes
from the word "knurd", which is "drunk" spelled back-
wards. What we know for certain is that word "nerd" first
appeared in print in a story by the American children's
writer, Dr Seuss, in 1950. **TIL**.'

TL;DR: Too Long; Didn't Read

What It Means: 'keep it short and sweet'. Not so easy for
some of us. I have a problem with prolixity. I say too
much. I once held the record for making the world's
longest-ever after-dinner speech: it lasted twelve and a
half hours. I'm not good at concise emails either. I don't
use three words when thirty will do. This is a mistake. Say
too much and the response will be **TL;DR** or, from
those in a real hurry, **TLDR**. President Trump, who
speaks to his people in tweets, has told his staff: 'I like
bullets or I like as little as possible. I don't need, you know,
200-page reports on something that can be handled on a

page.' Trump is in good company. During the Second World War, in August 1940, as the Battle of Britain was being fought in the skies above England, the prime minister, Winston Churchill, sent a note to his colleagues in government: 'To do our work, we all have to read a mass of papers. Nearly all of them are far too long. This wastes time, while energy has to be spent in looking for the essential points.' He believed that 'the discipline of setting out the real points concisely will prove an aid to clearer thinking'. Enough said.

Whoomp! There It Is

What It Means: hooray! '**Whoomp! (There It Is)**' began life as a song created by the Miami bass group, Tag Team, in 1993. Since then it has been covered and adapted by all sorts and used prolifically in films and at sporting events — and as an expression of triumph and joy in internet communication.

Wig

What It Means: an expression of delight: something that's so exciting it's literally blown your wig off. 'I've got a signed first edition of *Have You Eaten Grandma?* **Wig**!'

woot

What It Means: **woot** (spelled with a double-zero) is an internet interjection expressing joy, happiness, and delight. As **woot**, it is a **leetspeak** variant of the more prosaic 'woot'. It also appears as **whoot, wOOt, whoot, wewt,** and **wought**. (**Leet,** btw, also known as **1337** and **leetspeak** or **eleet**, is a system of modified spellings first

developed in the 1980s when people with pocket calcula-
tors made words out of the numbers that appeared on the
calculator screen. The word **leet** is also used as an adjective to describe genius performance, especially in the
world of online gaming.)

YMMV: Your Mileage May Vary

What It Means: 'your experience might not be quite the
same as mine'. '**YMMV**, but *Paddington 2* has to be one of
the great feel-good movies of all time. Not so *Phantom
Thread*.'

YOLO: You Only Live Once

What It Means: 'go for it!' **YOLO** as an acronym for
You Only Live Once has been around for genera-
tions, certainly since the 1937 Henry Fonda film of the
same name and certainly before the Canadian rapper
Drake popularised it by using it in his 2011 hit song, 'The
Motto'.

You use **YOLO** both to justify doing something weird
and wonderful and as an ironic comment on something that someone else might have dared to do, but
inadvisedly. 'I hear Gyles is doing an impression of
Drake singing "The Motto" in his new one-man show.
YOLO.'

zzZzz

What It Means: zzZzz is pronounced 'zee-zee-ZEE-zee-
zee' and means 'sleep' when spoken and 'sleeping' when
simply written as **zzzzz** or **ZZZZZ**. It can also mean
'boring'. **ZZZZZ**. End of.

End of

What It Means: what it says. '**End of**' is a shorthand phrase used to bring a discussion to a close and to assert that nothing more needs to be said on the matter. 'He's not my boyfriend. **End of.**'

9. Bad Language?

Dipping into urbandictionary.com or reading the lyrics of a world-class rapper like Drake, you come across a raft of words with which, I imagine, your great-grandmother would not have been familiar – or, if she was, would certainly not have used.

The 'N' word is not one of them. It's hard to imagine now, but my great-grandmother had a set of matching shoes, gloves, and handbag whose colour was described by the highly respectable store from which she bought them (Derry & Toms of Kensington High Street in London) as 'Nigger brown'. Her generation commonly used the phrase 'nigger in the woodpile'. And, in November 1939, Great-granny was one of many who lined up to buy what turned out to be Agatha Christie's most successful novel, entitled *Ten Little Niggers*. The book went on to sell 100 million copies and is the world's best-selling murder mystery.

The Christie novel has been renamed, of course: it's now known as *And Then There Were None*. If you're a rapper like Drake, you can use the 'N' word. If you're not black, you can't.

You can use 'black', however, to describe a person's colour and most authorities now agree that 'black' is the most generally acceptable term to use. The 'N' word is a derivative of the word 'negro' (from the Latin for 'black', *niger*), which was adopted from Spanish and Portuguese and first recorded in the sixteenth century. 'Negro' was the standard term used to describe the colour of a black person until the twentieth century and in America, for example, considered quite acceptable by early black civil rights campaigners like Booker T. Washington. With the rise of the Black Power movement in the 1960s, 'negro' fell out of favour and 'black' was preferred. Then in the US 'black', too, became taboo and 'African-American' came to the fore. Now, 'black' is back.

And, in both American and British English, 'black' is best. Awkward usages such as 'exotic', 'other', 'urban', and 'ethnic' should be kept out of the mix. 'Coloured' is totally unacceptable — and has been for a generation — though 'person of colour' is considered passable by many, as is 'of African or West Indian heritage' where appropriate.

What about people of mixed heritage like Meghan Markle and President Obama? Or Drake himself, whose father is black American (from Memphis, Tennessee) and whose mother is Ashkenazi Jewish Canadian (from Toronto, Ontario)?

According to Leah Donnella, a mixed heritage American graduate in Africana Studies who has done the research, there's 'a dizzying multitude' of mixed heritage monikers and synonyms in use around the world, many of which are offensive. She says:

'Skip ahead if you want to avoid some of the worst — otherwise, here we go: muwalladeen, mulattos, mestizos, mestiços, blended, biracial, interracial, multiracial, multiethnic, gray, high yellow, half-breed, mixed-breed, cross-breed, mutt, mongrel, mixed blood, mixed race, mixed heritage, quadroon, octoroon, hapa, pardo, sambo, half-cracker but a nigger, too. In early Rome, we were *di colore*, "of color." In Japan, we are mostly called *hāfu* (half) but sometimes we get to be *daburu* (double). We were half-castes in the U.K. until 2001 (2001!), when the census officially deemed us "mixed." In South Africa, we are coloured, officially, and unofficial "bushies," a slang term that comes from the idea that multiracial children are conceived in the bush. In Brazil, where multiraciality is assumed, the options are colourful: *cor de canela*, *cor de rosa*, *cor de crema*, *cor de burro quando foge* (the colour of a donkey as it runs away).'

For me, 'mixed heritage' does the job well enough.

The Brandreth Rule is simple: at all times avoid racist, sexist, homophobic, and transphobic language — and, when in doubt, err on the side of sensitivity. In my book, bigoted language, and language that can be perceived as bigoted, is bad language.

Okay, we can probably all agree on that, but what about rude words, crude words, and swear words? That's 'a different gether altothing', as the late Princess Margaret liked to say. Some people just love 'em and these days they are not easy to avoid. Call me old-fashioned (or unduly sensitive), but I don't like them in public places and, on the whole and as a rule, I do my best to avoid any language likely to offend. If you are with strangers, or people you don't know well, my advice would be: watch what you say and think before you fire off a string of four-letter expletives. Why upset people by using words and phrases that may make them feel embarrassed or uncomfortable?

I was still a schoolboy when, on 13 November 1965, the theatre critic, Kenneth Tynan, became the first person to say 'fuck' on British television. I heard it as it happened. My parents were embarrassed. The nation (or most of it) was scandalised; the BBC apologised; and the actress Miriam Margolyes popped up to say that it was actually she who had said it on TV first, as a frustrated aside when appearing on *University Challenge* in 1963. It turns out, in fact, that the Irish playwright Brendan Behan was probably the first person to first utter the ancient Anglo-Saxon expletive on the box when he appeared live on *Panorama* in 1956, but it wasn't properly noticed at the time because he was so drunk he was slurring most of what he had to say.

'Fuck' on TV no longer causes a scandal, but it is still distressing to many. And broadcasters, rightly, are aware of that. If you want guidance on what is and isn't acceptable in terms of bad language today, I don't think you can do much better than the BBC Editorial Guidelines on the matter:

> 'Strong language' is language that has the potential to offend. It is not possible to compile a definitive list of strong words. Language is fluid, with new words and phrases regularly entering the public vocabulary. Also, the power of established terms to offend may change over time. For example, racist abuse or pejorative terms relating to physical or mental illness and sexual orientation have become increasingly unacceptable to audiences.

The BBC does not ban words or phrases. However, it is the responsibility of all content makers to ensure strong language is used only where it is editorially justified. The acceptability of language to intended audiences should be judged with care. If in doubt consult a senior editorial figure within your department or Editorial Policy.

The strongest language, with the potential to cause most offence, includes terms such as **cunt, motherfucker** and **fuck** (which are subject to mandatory referrals to Output Controllers); others such as **cocksucker** and **nigger** are also potentially extremely offensive to audiences.

Language that can cause moderate offence includes terms such as **wanker, pussy, bastard, slag**, etc. Care should be taken with using such terms; they may generate complaints if used in pre-watershed programmes on television [i.e. pre-9.00 p.m.] or in radio or online content and will require clear editorial justification if their use is to be supported.

Language that can cause mild offence includes **crap, knob, prat, tart** etc. These terms are unlikely to cause widespread offence when set against generally accepted standards if they are used sparingly and on their own. However, they should not be used indiscriminately.

Additionally, words or names associated with religion, such as **Jesus Christ**, may cause offence to some, but they are unlikely to cause widespread offence according to generally accepted standards. Again, we should still take care to avoid indiscriminate use.

I reckon that gets the balance about right. When it comes to bad language, my advice would be: treat your public the way the BBC aims to treat its.

My parents were born a long time ago (in 1910 and 1914) and I never heard either of them swear. In exasperation my mother might sometimes say 'blast' and my father would be guilty of the occasional 'damn', but nothing worse. If he said 'bloody' it was once in a blue moon.

Famously, Philip Larkin (born in 1922) began his poem, 'This Be The Verse' like this:

> They fuck you up, your mum and dad.
> They may not mean to, but they do.
> They fill you with the faults they had
> And add some extra, just for you.

My poem about my parents would begin a little differently:

> They tuck you up, your mum and dad ...

simply because that's what mine did. They tucked me up at night, read me stories, taught me poems, and gave me my love of language. Because of them, I don't swear very much. If my father hit his thumb with a hammer, he might say 'ouch'. I'd probably say 'fuck'. But it's not a word I use very often.

As a rule, I avoid the 'C' word altogether. It may have been around for seven hundred years, but it is still considered offensive by many. That said, it can occasionally be used to good effect. The other day I was rereading the diaries of the great theatre director Sir Peter Hall and came across a story about two actors of note, Dinsdale Landen (1932–2003) and Sir Donald Wolfit. Wolfit (1902–68), an actor-manager of the old school, was famous for touring the United Kingdom, playing all the leading Shakespearean roles.

Dinsdale Landen told today a wonderful story of his days as assistant stage manager at Worthing [in 1952]. He was a walk-on when Wolfit was there as guest star, playing Othello, but was not told what to do until the dress rehearsal, at which the great man said it would be a very good idea for Othello to have a page who followed him everywhere. He handed Dinsdale a loin cloth, told him to black-up, and said he'd got the part. Dinsdale did not know the play and just went wherever Wolfit went, the complete dutiful page, always in attendance. But at one point he found himself in a scene in which he felt rather ill at ease; he had an instinct about it. Suddenly he heard the great man's voice roaring, 'Not in Desdemona's bedroom, you cunt.'

Innocent Words That Sound Rude

If you like rude words (and some people do), English is awash with place names designed to lift your spirits. Here are a few of my favourites:

Bachelor's Bump, East Sussex
Backside Lane, Oxfordshire
Beaver Close, Surrey

Bedlam Bottom, Hampshire
Boggy Bottom, Abbots Langley, Hertfordshire
Brown Willy, Cornwall
Bushygap, Northumberland
Clap Hill, Kent
Cock Lane, Tutts Clump, Berkshire
Cockermouth, Cumbria
Crotch Crescent, Oxford
Deans Bottom, Kent
Dicks Mount, Suffolk
Faggot, Northumberland
Fanny Avenue, Derbyshire
Fanny Barks, Durham
Feltham Close, Hampshire
Gravelly Bottom Road, near Langley Heath, Kent
Great Cockup and Little Cockup
   (hills in the Lake District), Cumbria
Grope Lane, Shropshire
Happy Bottom, Dorset
Honey Knob Hill, Wiltshire
Honeypot Lane, Leicestershire
Hooker Road, Norwich
Juggs Close, East Sussex
Knockerdown, Derbyshire
Minge Lane, Worcestershire
Nob End, Lancashire
Ogle Close, Merseyside
Old Sodbury, Gloucestershire
Old Sodom Lane, Wiltshire
Pratt's Bottom, Kent
Sandy Balls, Hampshire

Scratchy Bottom, Dorset
Shaggs, Dorset
Shittington, Bedfordshire
Slack Bottom, West Yorkshire
Slag Lane, Merseyside
Spanker Lane, Derbyshire
Thong, Kent
Titty Hill, West Sussex
Titty Ho, Northamptonshire
Ugley, Essex
Wash Dyke, Norfolk
Wetwang, East Yorkshire
Wham Bottom Lane, Lancashire
Willey, Warwickshire
Winkle Street, Southampton
Wyre Piddle, Worcestershire

And a friend who works on the *Oxford English Dictionary* sent me this list of entirely innocent foreign words that sound amusingly rude to English ears:

Biche
It's French for 'doe'

Fahrt
It's German and it means a 'journey', 'ride', or 'trip'
(Tony Blair's 2010 autobiography was called *A Journey*.
In Germany it was called *Ein Fahrt*)

Prick
It's Swedish for a 'dot' or a 'spot'

Dick
It's German for 'thick'

Coque
It's French for 'seashell'
(not to be confused with *coq* which is French for
'cock' and reminds us of Victoria Wood's classic
translation of *coq au vin* as 'love in a lorry')

Kant
It's Dutch for 'side', 'edge', 'border'

Phoque
It's French for the animal, the seal

Faca
It's Portuguese for 'knife'

Slagroom
It's Dutch and means 'whipped cream'

Slutspurt
It's Swedish for 'end', 'finish'

Is Slanguage Bad Language?

My father was fond of a muffin. The muffin he liked was
the quintessential English tea-time treat: a flat circular
spongy bread roll made from yeast dough and eaten split,
toasted, and generously buttered. That's the only kind of

'muffin' you'd find listed in an English dictionary when I was a boy. Now 'muffin' has become a slang term for all sorts of things, including the roll of fat around your midriff ('muffin-top'), the female private parts, and an attractive person. The word can even be used as a verb, as in the old joke: 'Do you like Muffin the Mule? No, I prefer Dobbin the Donkey.'

According to the American poet Carl Sandburg, slang is 'a language that rolls up its sleeves, spits on its hands and goes to work'. According to the dictionary on my desk, slang is 'a type of language consisting of words and phrases that are regarded as very informal, are more common in speech than writing, and are typically restricted to a particular context or group of people'. According to the online Urban Dictionary, 'British slang isn't the same as the olden days. We don't still say stuff like "jolly good show" and eat cucumber sandwiches, unless you are quite posh. We do still say "bloody hell" quite a lot though. Mostly it is stuff like: innit, chav, well good, brill, mingin', wkd etc.'

'Innit', 'brill', 'wkd' are short for 'isn't it', 'brilliant', and 'wicked' — which means 'wonderful' not 'wicked'. 'Mingin'', intriguingly, has been around since the 1950s and means something 'unpleasant and well past its sell-by date'. 'Chav' is more recent, dating from the turn of the twenty-first century, and according to one of the contributors to the Urban Dictionary:

Male chavs wear clothes and jewellry which come from a market, they have a attitude problem and smoke since the age of 11.

Female chavs wear tight trousers and when they sit down they're thongs show, have fake blonde hair as straight as an ironing board or they have the 'croydon face-lift', they lost their virginity at the age of 14, they have a attitide problem and they have really really bad teeth.

Chavs also use stupid words such as 'safe' or 'mint' or 'y'wot?' or 'quali'ee' or my favourite 'innit' what are they trying to say?, it's like trying to communicate with a dog.

you usually find them in your local bus stop or your local town. [*Sic.*[32]]

A 'Croydon facelift' is a woman's hairstyle where the hair is pulled back tightly and tied in a bun or ponytail at the back. (In Northern Ireland it's known as a 'Millie facelift'.) 'Safe' and 'mint' are synonyms for 'cool'. 'Cool', of course, is what used to be 'hot'. Slang is ever-evolving. While an Edwardian dandy might have wooed his dimpled darling with lovey-dovey terms of endearment, a modern Romeo might use a more contemporary line in flattery: 'Bae, you is one cool, sick, mean bitch.'

---

[32] *Sic* is a Latin adverb meaning 'thus' or 'just as' and stands for *sic erat scriptum*, 'thus was it written'. You insert it in square brackets, as I have done, after a quoted word or passage to indicate that what you have quoted has been transcribed *exactly* as in the original and that you're aware it contains errors but are forced to keep them in for the purposes of historical accuracy.

The Wonder of Wodehouse

What ho! The dudes at the online Urban Dictionary are right: British slang isn't what it once was. Incidentally, 'dude' meaning 'a cool guy' is an older term than you might think: it dates from the late nineteenth century and is reckoned to be shortened from 'doodle' as in 'Yankee Doodle Dandy'. 'Posh', interestingly, originated as a noun, meaning someone who was a 'dude' or a 'dandy'. It gradually morphed into an adjective to describe someone from the upper classes, but there is no evidence to support the idea that 'posh' comes from the initials of 'port out, starboard home', referring to the more comfortable accommodation, out of the heat of the sun, on the ships travelling between England and India at the height of the British Empire.

People seem to think I'm 'posh' because of the way I speak. In fact, I'm solid English middle class, but I sound the way I do because I sound exactly like my father and he sounded like every other English professional person of his generation. Over the years I have done my best to modify my accent so that I sound less plummy than I used to do. Once in a while I see a clip of myself on TV from the 1960s and 1970s. It's horrific: I make Jacob Rees-Mogg look like the Artful Dodger.

My father was learning to speak, and read and write, in the teens and twenties of the twentieth century, at exactly the time the great P. G. Wodehouse was publishing his early novels and introducing readers to the wonderful world of Jeeves and his master, Bertie Wooster. Pelham

Grenville Wodehouse (known to his chums as 'Plum') incorporated the upper-class slang of the time into his novels and invented or popularised a string of slang words and phrases. He turned an everyday noun like 'ankle' into an evocative verb: 'Bertie ankled down to the club.' He is credited with coming up with 'plonk' as the word for setting something down heavily and 'pottiness' for something that's daft. Among his other gems were:

'bally' meaning 'bloody'
'crispish' meaning 'somewhat crisp'
'gruntled', as opposed to 'disgruntled',
meaning 'contented'
'nosebag' to indicate food
'oojah-cum-spiff', meaning 'all right' or 'fine'
'rannygazoo', meaning 'fuss' or 'bother'
'rummy', meaning 'odd' or 'strange'
'snooter', a verb meaning 'to harass' or 'snub'
'zing', an interjection announcing the arrival of
something unexpected

His slang synonyms for being the worse the wear for drink included being:

awash
boiled
fried
illuminated
lathered
oiled
ossified

pie-eyed
polluted
primed
scrooched
stinko
squiffy
tanked
tiddly
and (my favourite) woozled

In the slanguage of Wodehouse, 'What ho!' is the favoured form of greeting — as in *My Man Jeeves* (1919):

> 'What ho!' I said.
> 'What ho!' said Motty.
> 'What ho! What ho!'
> 'What ho! What ho! What ho!'
> After that it seemed rather difficult to go on
>   with the conversation.

And 'Tootle-oo!' is what you say when you want to say 'goodbye', to which the correct slang response is 'pip-pip'.
    Cheerio.

Cockney Rhyming Slang

The world is awash with slanguages. You find them in the works of Wodehouse, in schools, in colleges, in prisons, in street gangs. You find them in particular communities and parts of a country. In the London of the 1980s, the so-called

'Sloane Rangers' (braying posh types at home in the streets around Sloane Square) and 'Yuppies' ('Young Urban Professionals') had a language of their own. In the world of contemporary rap and rock, they speak a special way. (When will.i.am first appeared on British television, I was hired by the BBC to provide simultaneous translation.) Slanguages come and go: some are more interesting than others, but I don't think any of them constitute 'bad language'.

One of the of the oldest, most celebrated, and longest-surviving English-language slangs is Cockney Rhyming Slang. Dating from the 1840s and originating in the East End of London,[33] nobody knows for sure how it evolved. Here, for a bubble bath, are 101 of my favourite Cockney Rhyming Slang words and phrases — some Victorian (like 'plates of meat' for 'feet'), some much more recent (like 'Lionel Blairs' for 'flares'). Many of the words derive from the popular culture of the era in which they became part of Rhyming Slang. Lionel Blair is a British dancer and choreographer; Vera Lynn was 'the Forces' sweetheart' during the Second World War; Bob Hope was an American comedian; Tommy Trinder was a British one; Alan Whicker was a British TV reporter; Mork and Mindy were US sitcom characters played by Robin Williams and Pam Dawber; Ruby Murray was a Northern Irish singer popular in the 1950s; Tod Sloan was an American jockey, famous at the beginning of the twentieth century.

---

[33] A true Cockney is someone born within earshot of the bells of St Mary-le-Bow church in the City of London — which, for purists, means there have been no Cockneys born since the Second World War when the bells were destroyed by German bombing.

Sometimes in Cockney Slang the full phrase is reduced, so that 'having a butcher's' is said instead of 'having a butcher's hook', meaning 'having a look', or 'use your loaf' is said instead of 'use your loaf of bread' to mean 'use your head'. 'Would you Adam and Eve it? She came down the apples and pears without her Alan Whickers, and met the Artful Dodger on the landing. He was going for a laugh 'n' a joke, but stayed to have a butcher's. That led to a Barney.' You get the idea.

1. Adam and Eve — believe
2. Alan Whickers — knickers
3. Apples and Pears — stairs
4. Aris (short for 'Aristotle') — bottle
5. Artful Dodger — lodger
6. Ascot Races — braces
7. Baked Bean — queen
8. Baker's Dozen — cousin
9. Ball and Chalk — walk
10. Barnaby Rudge — judge
11. Barnet Fair — hair
12. Barney Rubble — trouble
13. Battlecruiser — boozer
14. Bees and Honey — money
15. Bird Lime — time (in prison)
16. Biscuits and Cheese — knees
17. Boat Race — face
18. Bob Hope — soap
19. Boracic (short for 'boracic lint') — skint
20. Bottle and Glass — arse (confidence)
21. Brahms and Liszt — pissed (drunk)

22. Brass Tacks — facts
23. Bread and Cheese — sneeze
24. Bread and Honey — money
25. Bricks and Mortar — daughter
26. Bristol City — breast
27. Brown Bread — dead
28. Bubble and Squeak — Greek
29. Bubble Bath — laugh
30. Butcher's Hook — look
31. Chalk Farm — arm
32. China Plate — mate (friend)
33. Cock and Hen — ten
34. Cows and Kisses — missus (wife)
35. Crust of Bread — head
36. Currant Bun — sun (also the *Sun* newspaper)
37. Custard and Jelly — telly (television)
38. Daffadowndilly — silly
39. Daisy Roots — boots
40. Darby and Joan — moan
41. Dicky Bird — word
42. Dinky Doos — shoes
43. Dog and Bone — phone
44. Duck and Dive — skive
45. Duke of Kent — rent
46. Dustbin Lid — kid
47. Elephant's Trunk — drunk
48. Fireman's Hose — nose
49. Flowery Dell — cell
50. Frog and Toad — road
51. Gypsy's Kiss — piss
52. Half-Inch — pinch (to steal)

53. Hampton Wick — prick
54. Irish Pig — wig
55. Jam-Jar — car
56. Jimmy Riddle — piddle
57. Joanna — piano (pronounced 'pianna')
58. Khyber Pass — arse
59. Kick and Prance — dance
60. Lady Godiva — fiver
61. Laugh 'n' a Joke — smoke
62. Lionel Blairs — flares
63. Loaf of Bread — head
64. Loop the Loop — soup
65. Mickey Bliss — piss
66. Mince Pies — eyes
67. Mork and Mindy — windy
68. North and South — mouth
69. Orchestra Stalls — balls
70. Pat and Mick — sick
71. Peckham Rye — tie
72. Plates of Meat — feet
73. Pony and Trap — crap
74. Rabbit and Pork — talk
75. Raspberry Ripple — nipple
76. Raspberry Tart — fart
77. Roast Pork — fork
78. Rosy Lee — tea (drink)
79. Round the Houses — trousers
80. Rub-a-Dub — pub
81. Ruby Murray — curry
82. Sausage Roll — goal
83. Septic Tank — Yank

84. Sherbet (short for 'sherbet dab') — cab (taxi)
85. Skin and Blister — sister
86. Sky Rocket — pocket
87. Sweeney Todd — Flying Squad
88. Syrup of Figs — wig
89. Tables and Chairs — stairs
90. Tea Leaf — thief
91. Tod Sloan — alone
92. Tom and Dick — sick
93. Tom Tit — shit
94. Tomfoolery — jewellery
95. Tommy Trinder — window
96. Trouble and Strife — wife
97. Two and Eight — state (upset)
98. Uncle Bert — shirt
99. Vera Lynn — gin
100. Weasel and Stoat — coat
101. Whistle and Flute — suit (of clothes)

So Annoying, Like

I'm with Carl Sandburg. I quite like slang. What I don't like is, er, 'like' …

I was on the bus yesterday and overheard a teenage schoolboy tell his friend: 'I was like a bit late like, not like a lot late like, just a bit like late, but he like just went like ballistic, you know like, really like totally mad. It was terrible like.'

It is terrible like the way 'like' has become the go-to linguistic filler of our times. It's not the only one, of course.

There's 'um' and 'er' and 'I mean', as well: sounds, words, and phrases that serve no useful purpose, get in the way of what you want to say, and can be very, *very* irritating.

Listening to the *Today* programme on BBC Radio 4 this morning, every one of eight consecutive interviewees began their first answer with either the word 'Well' or the word 'So'. It's so annoying — and, well, unnecessary.

In my book, bad language includes the words we use all the time, but don't need to — like 'like' and 'I mean' between every other word, and 'well' and 'so' at the start of every sentence. I am also tired of the fashionable words that, while useful when apposite, have become debased through overuse: 'iconic', 'nuanced', 'stakeholders', 'authentic', and 'passionate' are five of my particular bugbears. These days, maintaining the current 'discourse' (another horror) appears impossible without them.

Different overused words and phrases annoy different people. On the Channel 4 words-and-numbers game *Countdown*, contestants have to ask one of the presenters, Rachel Riley, to select their letters and numbers for them. Before the recording the contestants are given written guidance which states: 'When requesting letters or numbers from Rachel, please avoid using the expression "Can I get" as it generates a large number of complaints from viewers.' Of course it does. It drives them mad. It drives *me* mad. My children do it in restaurants. 'Can I get the chorizo?' they say. I suppose they could go out to the kitchen to get it, but that's generally not the way the system works. 'Can I have?' or 'May I have?' is correct. 'Can I get?' is wrong, wrong, WRONG.

Here is my catalogue of the most annoying words and

turns of phrase in current usage. You'll have your own. These are mine. Basically (yes, that's another one), I've had enough of them.

I'm good
Really?

That's so random
Is it?

Whatever
Go away

Have a nice day
You said that without thinking, didn't you?

Do you know what?
I'm about to find out, aren't I?

Back in the day
What's wrong with 'once' or 'in the past'?

Going forward
What's wrong with 'from now on' or 'in future'?

Upcoming
What's wrong with 'forthcoming'?

Tick all the boxes
Must you?

Speaking personally
Must you?

I, personally
Who else is there?

I have to say
Do you?

Gutted
I hope not

I was sat
Don't you mean, 'I was sitting'?

I was stood
Don't you mean, 'I was standing'?

Absolutely
What's wrong with 'yes'?

Met with
What's wrong with 'met'?

Cook down / Boil off
What's wrong with 'cook' and 'boil'?

Oftentimes
What's wrong with 'often'?

Ahead of
I think you mean 'before'

Go figure
No thank you

Comfortable in their own skins
Who else's skins were they going to be in?

Keep calm and ...
*Stop! It was fun to start with: now it's just another
overused cliché*

Kickstart
What's wrong with 'start'?

Cray, cray
I think the word is 'crazy'

Filling forms out
*You fill them **in**, don't you?*

HR
*Are humans really 'resources'? What was wrong
with 'personnel'?*

Safe haven
If it's a haven, it's safe

Blue-sky thinking
Oh dear

Don't go there
Now I really want to

Let's be absolutely clear
'I'm about to muddy the waters'

To be absolutely honest with you
I don't believe you!

Forward planning
As opposed to 'backward planning'?

Step up to the plate
What's all that about?

Park up
What's wrong with 'park'?

Pre-planned
I think you mean 'planned'

Pushback
Do you miss 'resist'?

Fashionista
Not in vogue

Factor in
What's wrong with 'include'?

From the get-go
What's wrong with 'the start'?

Outside of
We don't need that 'of', thank you

Off of
*As in 'I got off of the table' — we don't need that
'of' either, thanks*

Are you all right there?
Did you mean, 'May I help you?'

We need to call them out
What exactly do you mean?

No offence, but …
'Warning: I'm about to be offensive'

See you later
But you're never going to see me again

Specialty
The word is 'speciality'

It is what it is
Is it really?

With all due respect
I have none for you, that's a given

Irregardless
I think you mean 'regardless', but perhaps you mean 'irrespective'?

Pacifically
I think you mean 'specifically'

Partially
I think you mean 'partly'
('Partially' means taking sides, as opposed to 'impartially')

Referencing
Do you mean 'referring to'?

Just saying
Do you have to?

Ballpark figure
Where or what's a 'ballpark'?

Lockdown
Where's that come from?

Bang on trend
So last year

Completely unique
'Unique' is all you need

What's not to like?
A great deal

Where it's at
Where's that exactly?

Aficionado
What do you know, really?

I've a window in my diary
I'm looking out on to the garden through mine

My bad
Not good

I have to say …
Oh no, you don't

I hear what you're saying
But I'm not really listening

Totes
Don't you mean 'totally'?

Listen up
Do you mean 'listen' or 'pay attention'?

Free gift
*Yup, it's free: it's a gift: it doesn't
need to be both*

Pre-order
If you've paid for it, you've ordered it

Political grandee
Ah, either someone you've never heard of or someone who's past it

Celebrity
Someone you've never heard of

Should of
I think you mean 'Should have'

For free
It's either 'free' or it isn't

At this moment in time
'Now'

At the end of the day
When's that exactly?

Take it to the next level
Do we have to?

Sorry, not sorry
Please – spare me!

No-brainer
You said it

Awesomesauce
That's even worse than 'Amazeballs'

Wow! Just wow!
Enough already

You owned it
Oh no!

You nailed it
No! No!

Literally
No! No! No!

To die for
Really?

Your call is important to us
Fuck off

I cannot stand being 'kept on the line' while they play ghastly music at me, interrupted by mini 'product promotions' and an irritating voice telling me that the conversation — which I am failing to have — may be recorded 'for training purposes'. And, just while I'm in full 'rant' mode, can I say, particularly because I'm British and not American, I also can't stand it when people pronounce 'controversy' as 'conTRO-Versy', 'secretary' as 'sekketary', 'library' as 'libary', 'regularly' as 'reggaly', 'schedule' as 'skedule', 'harassment' as 'haRASS-ment', 'spontaneity' as 'spontanAity', 'Antarctic' as 'Antartic', 'barbiturate' as 'barbituate', 'February' as 'Febyary', 'espresso' as 'expresso', and 'et cetera' as 'excetera'. 'Mischievous' is 'mis-che-vus' not 'mis-che-vee-us'. 'LEEverage' is correct

'LEV Verage' is not. And 'H' is 'aitch' not 'haitch', but you knew that.

Surveys suggest that in recent years the overused word that has annoyed most people the most is 'whatever'. A 2018 survey has 'fake news' and 'huge' jostling for top spot in the Most Irritating Words List, possibly reflecting President Trump's fondness for using them in his tweets to his tweeps. (Your 'tweeps' are your Twitter followers.) In the UK, according to the survey, people have had enough of 'thinking outside the box' and looking for 'a level playing field'. In the US, they are tiring of 'lit' (instead of 'intoxicated'), 'keep it 100' (instead of 'tell the truth', 'keep it real'), and 'woke' (meaning 'being aware', especially when it comes to issues of social justice).

Almost any phrase wears thin with overuse. The 1999 movie *Fight Club* gave a new meaning to the word 'snowflake' when it had one of its characters say: 'You are not special. You're not a beautiful and unique snowflake. You're the same decaying organic matter as everything else.' 'Snowflake' became a term used to describe self-regarding and over-sensitive young people, prone to taking offence and liable to melt like snowflakes when the going gets even slightly hot. I reckon we are wearying of 'snowflake' now. I had certainly wearied of 'thinking outside the box' until last year when I was invited to host the British Funeral Directors' Awards and found that the main prize of the night was for 'thinking outside the box'. I liked that. I also liked the prize for the Crematorium of the Year: the 'Crem de la crem' award.

In my book, anything that smacks of predictability and pretentiousness counts as bad language. I went to a meeting at one of the world's largest advertising agencies recently and heard the team there talking about 'journeys', 'narratives', 'emotional engagement', and 'vertiginous game-changers'. They told me, in all seriousness, they weren't 'advertising people': they were 'story-tellers'. Amazebonk.

Ad Nausea

While I'm having a go at the ad people, can I say how much I abhor this sort of usage:

Eat colourful
Dress beautiful
Work easy
Travel safe

Get lost.

And I deprecate the modern fad for adding a 'y' to adjectives that don't require one. Toast that was once 'crisp' is now 'crispy'; an Emma Bridgewater teapot that was 'dotted' is now 'dotty'. It's a 'slippy' slope as far as I'm concerned.

Tautology Torture

On the early train to Edinburgh yesterday, just before we were due to depart, the guard said: 'If you're not intending to travel, please return back to the platform.' That troubled me all the way from King's Cross to York. We didn't need that 'back'. 'Tautology' is unnecessary repetition — like:

return back
climb up
fall down

'Tautology' is saying the same thing twice — unnecessarily. It's not 'a PIN number', it's 'a PIN' because 'PIN' stands for 'Personal Identification Number': you've already included the number once. The same goes for 'ATM machine' and 'HIV virus': the 'machine' and the 'virus' are already there because the initials stand for 'Automated Teller Machine' and 'Human Immunodeficiency Virus'.

Other everyday tautological horrors include:

absolute certainty
added bonus
awful tragedy
close scrutiny
complete opposite
end result
factual information
final conclusion
honest truth
new innovation
sum total
terrible disaster
unconfirmed rumour

You can say 'almost unique' because something might indeed be *almost* unique' if, say, there are two of them in the universe, not just one. But 'totally unique' is totally wrong. Unique *is* unique. To say 'they arrived one after the other in succession' is wrong — but to say 'they arrived one after the other in quick succession' is acceptable, because you are doing more than repeat what you have just said: you are adding extra information.

Euphemism, to Put It Mildly

In 1945, Emperor Hirohito of Japan, after two atomic bombs, the loss of 3 million people and with invasion imminent, informed his subjects of their country's unconditional surrender. He told them, 'The war situation has developed not necessarily to Japan's advantage.'

A 'euphemism', according to the dictionary on my desk, is 'the substitution of a mild, indirect or vague term for one considered to be harsh, offensive, embarrassing or distressing'. Some euphemisms are well intentioned; some are designed to mislead. If kindness or courtesy are the motivation for a euphemism, that's one thing. If distortion and deception are the motivating factors, that's quite another. Before you use a euphemism, think carefully about why you're using it.

In his 1948 novel, *Nineteen Eighty-Four*, George Orwell introduced us to the concepts of 'doublethink' and 'newspeak'. Three years earlier, in his polemic, 'Politics and the English Language', he warned us about the language of politicians designed 'to make lies sound truthful and murder respectable'. This was some years before we became accustomed to hearing about 'enhanced interrogation techniques' (*aka* 'systematic torture of detainees'), 'collateral damage' ('death of civilians who got in the way'), and 'neutralised zones' ('we got rid of the bastards').

We now know that politicians who 'misspeak' or come up with 'a terminological inexactitude' are not just being 'economical with the truth': they've lied. If at work you hear the words 'career change', 'transition opportunity', 'personnel realignment', 'right-sizing', 'down-sizing', or 'workforce re-engineering', watch out: they're about to 'let you go', give you the chance 'to pursue other interests', and 'spend more time with your family'. You're fired!

But don't worry. As a consequence, you won't go broke. You may suffer a 'temporary negative cash-flow', you may have to trade in your new car for one that has been 'pre-loved', or even sell your house (it's 'an underperforming asset' after all), but nobody is 'poor' any more. They are simply 'economically disadvantaged'. Here's hoping you don't have to move to 'an economically depressed neighbourhood' in 'a culturally deprived environment'. It's bound to be a shithole.

We live in a world of euphemisms, where 'partially proficient' means 'useless', 'adult' means 'pornographic', 'curvy' means 'fat', 'voluptuous' means 'fatter', 'chubby' means 'obese', and 'senior' means you're virtually dead.

Never Say Die

Have you noticed how, nowadays, nobody dies? They 'pass away' or — worse — they simply 'pass', as if they can't think of an answer on *Mastermind*. 'Never say die' seems to be the motto of our times.

I don't like 'passing' as a euphemism for 'dying'. To me it feels excessively namby-pamby. Of the many alternatives, these are my favourites. When I 'go west' and am 'pushing up the daisies', feel free to say he ...

popped his clogs
breathed his last
cashed in his chips
fell off the perch
pegged out
gave up the ghost
met the Grim Reaper
kicked the bucket
bit the dust
shuffled off this mortal coil
snuffed it
croaked
went to his just reward

Or, best of all, 'assumed room temperature'.

Toilet Talk

What do you call it?

The toilet
The lavatory
The loo
The WC
The bathroom
The powder room
The rest room

The comfort station
The little boys' room / the little girls' room
Ladies / Gents
The smallest room
The washroom
The facilities
The outhouse
The crapper
The potty
The john
The can
The privy
The latrine
The jakes
The necessarium
The lavvy
The excretorium
The urination station
The sandbox
The khazi
The bog
The netty
The shithouse

And what do you do when you get there?

Have a pee
Have a piddle
Powder your nose
Wash your hands
Do your business

Have a tinkle
Talk to a man about a horse
Point Percy at the porcelain
Steer Stanley to the stainless steel
Let Letty loose
Spend a penny
Squeeze the lemon
Shake hands with the vicar
Talk to grandma slowly
Shake the water off the lily
Drain the dragon
Drain the radiator
Drain the one-eyed monster
Make the bladder gladder
Syphon the python
Park your breakfast
Drop a load
A Number One
A Number Two

Too much information? I agree, but it's still an issue. Samuel Pepys called his jakes 'the House of Office'. The Queen, brought up to call it 'the lavatory' or 'the loo', has been heard to call it 'the toilet' in recent years, probably because that's the term favoured by her grandchildren's generation. If you want guidance on the matter, I suggest you can't do better than follow the Queen's example. That's what I do.

Some years ago, when I was writing a book about the Queen and Prince Philip, and given the opportunity to travel with the royal couple when they went about their official duties, I wondered how Her Majesty's 'comfort breaks' would be described in the detailed schedule of her day supplied to the police and the local Lord Lieutenant. Would it be: '12 noon: the Royal Wee'? '12 noon: HM on the throne'? No. It was simpler and much more decorous: '12 noon: Opportunity to tidy.'

Sex

Sex has been around as long as we have (natch), and euphemisms for having sex have been in existence as far back as recorded language goes. I thought I would include an A to Z of euphemisms for sexual intercourse, running from 'act of darkness' to 'zig-zagging', but when I discovered that there are well over a thousand to choose from I thought better of it. Instead, I am offering you fifteen of my historic favourites. 'Making love', 'sleeping with', 'humping', and 'shagging' are all much older turns of phrase than you might think. But you already know those. These are more evocative.

Give Someone a Green Gown
From the 1300s
This term refers to having sex outdoors on the grass

The Service of Venus
From the 1390s
Venus was the Roman goddess of love

Playing Nug-a-Nug
From the 1500s

Make Butter with Your Tail
From the 1590s

Make the Beast with Two Backs
From the 1590s
Made famous by Shakespeare, as used by Iago in *Othello*

Shoot twixt Wind and Water
From the 1600s

Pierce the Hogshead
From the 1600s

Dance the Paphian Jig
From the 1650s
Paphos on Cyprus was sacred to Aphrodite, the Greek
goddess of love

Take a Turn among the Cabbages
From the 1700s

Make Feet for Children's Stockings
From the 1780s

Have Your Corn Ground
From the 1800s

Take a Turn in Bushey Park
From the 1800s
Bushey Park was a well-known trysting spot in
nineteenth-century London.

Put Four Quarters on the Spit
From the 1800s

Horizontal Refreshment
From the 1840s

Make Whoopee
From the 1920s

Netflix and Chill
From 2018

Job Description

If, like me, you work at the BBC, you won't regard the Corporation's satirical sitcom, *W1A*, as anything other than a fly-on-the-wall documentary series — and one that pulls its punches at that. In the real world, the BBC's Head of Vision may have gone and the Controller of Knowledge Commissioning may have been replaced; but when I last looked, the job descriptions at the BBC really did include a Head of Strategic Change, a Head of Talent and Change, and a Director of Transformation.

There's nothing new about pretentious job descriptions. In Victorian times, there were journalists who liked to call themselves 'couranteers' and swimming teachers who advertised their services as 'delineators of natatorial science'. I don't advocate calling a cleaner a 'hygiene technician', or the person who delivers your newspaper a 'media distribution officer', but now that the fire service includes women as well as men, it makes sense to call them 'firefighters' instead of 'firemen'.

Some actresses prefer to be called 'actors', which is fine, of course, but can cause confusion. The *Guardian* determined that the word 'actress' should always be replaced by the term 'actor' and surprised its readers in 2007 when it reported the death of Carlo Ponti, the Italian film producer and husband of Sophia Loren, with the words: 'Carlo Ponti, already a man with a good eye for pretty actors ...'

When it comes to political correctness, the Brandreth Rule is: use your common sense and get the balance right. I'm happy to think of Florence Nightingale as 'a heroine'. That's what she was in her time. As far as I'm concerned, she does not need to be 'a hero' now. But I'm equally happy for the person chairing the meeting to be called 'a chairman' (if male), 'a chairwoman' (if female), 'a chairperson', or 'a chair'. The era of the 'air hostess' is over: it makes total sense that, regardless of gender, we call them 'flight attendants' now. I don't go along with the recent academic report that claimed 'there is a danger PE lessons can contribute to a recolonisation of ethnic minorities' physicality' (that *was* 'political correctness gone mad'), but I do think it's preferable to say 'forebears' or 'ancestors' rather than 'forefathers', because that's what they were. That said, I wouldn't automatically replace 'motherhood' and 'fatherhood' with 'parenthood', because sometimes it is useful and necessary to be able to make a distinction. Language is about saying what you want to say, as clearly and precisely as you can. Some US newspaper style guides have banned the word 'gunman' and require 'shooter' to be used instead. But 'gunman' or 'gunwoman' each tells us more than 'shooter' would.

It's easy to have fun with political correctness:

Don't say 'alcoholic' — say 'anti-sobriety activist'

Don't say 'bald' — say 'follicularly challenged'

Don't say 'body odour' — say
'nondiscretionary fragrance'

Don't say 'cannibalism' — say 'intra-species dining'

Don't say 'clumsy' — say 'uniquely coordinated'

Don't say 'cowardly' — say 'challenge challenged'

Don't call them 'cowboys' — call them
'bovine control officers'

Don't call them 'dead' — say 'they're
metabolically challenged'

But language is power. Words do make a difference. They can reinforce stereotypes, cause offence, undermine, hurt, and humiliate. You don't have to wrap everything you say in cotton wool, but you should choose your words carefully. Good communication is about courtesy and kindness as well as clarity and getting your message across.

Don't Resist Change

The wilder excesses of political correctness I resist. I still call 'a lady' 'a lady' and, on the whole, she doesn't seem to mind. I still address a group of colleagues as 'you guys' because I think they know I'm regarding the girls in the group as guys, too, and, on the whole, they seem easy with that. What I don't do (or I try not to do) is use terms that I know may give offence just because they are terms my parents would have used and I want to insist on my right to use them, too. Nor do I resist some of the new words that the age of political correctness has thrust upon us. Many of them are intriguing — *viz*:

Cisgender

- Sometimes abbreviated to **cis**, it refers to people whose gender identity matches the gender they were assigned at birth. It's the opposite of **transgender**, of course, and has its root in the Latin prefix *cis-*, meaning 'on this side of'. *Trans-* comes from the Latin meaning 'on the other side of', 'across from'. **Cis** has spawned **cissexual**, **cissexism**, **cisnormativity**, and more beside.

Terf

- Sometimes written as **TERF**, because it's an acronym of **Trans-Exclusionary Radical Feminist**, it is best defined as a radical feminist who believes transsexual and transgender people do not have the right to consider themselves female. Not everyone is in sympathy with the **terfs**: according to the Rational Wiki website, they are a 'subgroup … characterised by **transphobia**, especially **transmisogyny**, and hostility to the **third wave of feminism**. They believe that the only real women are those born with a vagina and XX chromosomes. They wish to completely enforce the classic **gender binary**, supporting **gender essentialism**.'

The words we use reflect the world we live in. Language is one of the key keys to unlocking the secrets of any age. People are sometimes outraged to find certain words in the dictionary, but the dictionary-makers aren't there to pass judgement on our ever-evolving vocabulary: they are simply there to record it. And they tend not to record a new word or usage until they feel it's reasonably well-established. For example, 'cisgender' had been around a few years before making it into the *Oxford English Dictionary* in 2015 — alongside several hundred other new words and phrases, including:

Hot mess
Slang term for 'something or someone in extreme confusion or disorder'

Tenderpreneur
'A person who uses his or her political connections to secure government contracts and tenders for personal advantage', originating in South Africa

Carnap
Philippine English word meaning 'to steal a car'

Webisode
Short video, especially an instalment in a series, which is presented online rather than being broadcast on television

Presidentiable
'A person who is a likely or confirmed candidate for
president', from Philippine English

Once upon a time, it took years for Indian words — like
'bungalow', 'jodhpur', 'kedgeree', and 'hullabaloo' — to
be brought back to the capital of the British Empire and
assimilated into the English language. Now, thanks to television, the internet, and social media, new English words
from the Philippines and from Africa reach us instantly.
Our language reflects both globalisation and current
events. For example, following the surprise result of the
2017 British General Election and the higher-than-
expected turn-out of young people at the polls, the
Oxford Dictionaries Word of the Year for 2017 was:

Youthquake
'A significant cultural, political, or social change arising
from the actions or influence of young people'

Other 2017 'word of the year' contenders included:

Broflake
'[Derogatory, informal] a man who is readily upset or
offended by progressive attitudes that conflict with his
more conventional or conservative views'

Milkshake duck
'A person or thing that initially inspires delight on
social media but is soon revealed to have a distasteful or
repugnant past'

Newsjacking
'The practice of taking advantage of current events or news stories in such a way as to promote or advertise one's product or brand'

Unicorn
'Denoting something, especially an item of food or drink, that is dyed in rainbow colours, decorated with glitter, etc.'

From 'carnap' to 'newsjacking', many of our language's new words are portmanteau words, like 'twerk' (the dance that combines 'twist' and 'jerk') and 'Brexit' (from 'Britain' and 'exit') ... I wanted this book to be a Brexit-free zone, a safe space for believers and non-believers alike, so all I will say (and this is happily non-contentious) is that the word 'Brexit' has become the most rapidly recognised portmanteau word in history (blog has gone further, but not so fast) and possibly the most universally recognised one since 'brunch' (from 'breakfast' and 'lunch') came in to being in 1897. A 'portmanteau' is a large travelling bag, typically made of stiff leather and opening into two equal parts, and a 'portmanteau word' is one that combines two words and their meanings. Portmanteau words were pioneered by Lewis Carroll, who created 'chortle' ('chuckle' and 'snort') and 'galumph' ('gallop' and 'triumph'), among others.

As well as 'Brexit', other more recent portmanteau 'b' words include:

- **blog**, from 'web' and 'log'
- **botox**, from 'botulism' and 'toxin'

- **biopic**, from 'biography' and 'picture'
- **bootylicious**, from 'booty' and 'delicious'
- **Brangelina**, from 'Brad Pitt' and 'Angelina Jolie'
- **Britpop**, from 'British' and 'pop music'
- **bromance**, from 'bro' (brother) and 'romance'
- **Bruceploitation**, from 'Bruce Lee' and 'exploitation'
- **bankster**, from 'banker' and 'gangster'
- **banoffee**, from 'banana' and 'toffee'
- **bicurious**, from 'bisexual' and 'curious'
- **blaccent**, from 'black' and 'accent' — used by non-blacks who try to sound black
- **botel**, from 'boat' and 'hotel'
- **brainiac**, from 'brain' and 'maniac'
- **breathalyser**, from 'breath' and 'analyser'
- **burkini**, from 'burka' and 'bikini'

Like 'Brangelina', not all new words are built to last, but that doesn't mean to say you shouldn't enjoy them while they are around and relatively fresh. Language does not stand still and the use of language — grammar, spelling, and punctuation — won't stand still either. You cannot hold back change and resisting it dogmatically can make you very unhappy.

Change is important to our psychological well-being. This is something I learned a few years ago when I spent time with the eminent Irish psychiatrist Dr Anthony Clare. He had made a study of who gets to be happy, how, and why. He showed me research that indicated that people who are fearful of change are rarely happy. Dr Clare didn't advocate massive change, but enough to keep you stimulated. People are wary of change, particularly when things are going reasonably well, because they don't want to rock the boat; but apparently a little rocking can be good for us. Change is the salt in the soup of life.

Uniformity, it seems, is a tremendous threat to happiness, as are too much predictability and control and order. We need variety, flexibility, and the unexpected, because they challenge us. That's why we need new words and we need to be ready to embrace them. (That said, I do not want to learn another frigging password.)

Here's a random A to Z of new words, and words that have gained new meanings, in my lifetime. My grandparents wouldn't have understood even one of them:

Apple
As a child, it was just a fruit to me. Now I find I'm writing this book on one

Bootylicious
We are no longer allowed to tell anyone they're 'bootylicious', but we can *think* it all the same

Cankles
Chubby ankles and calves that lack definition and appear to merge

Charlie
To my grandparents 'Charlie' meant either Chaplin or a right fool; today 'Charlie' is either cocaine or the coolest dude you've ever met: your man

Detox
What you need if you've been overdoing the Charlie

Emoji

Frappuccino
'Frappuccino' is a trademarked brand of the Starbucks
Corporation for a line of iced, blended coffee drinks,
but, like 'Biro' and 'Hoover' before it, it's slipped
into our language

Gay
'Gay' used to mean 'light-hearted' and 'carefree': it still
does, but it also means 'homosexual' and has done, on
and off, since the end of the nineteenth century

Hoodie
Little Red Riding Hood was one of the first of them

Ill
'Ill' is good: something that's 'cool', 'tight', 'sweet', or
'sick' can also be described as 'ill'

Joint
What my grandparents once had for Sunday lunch
became a hand-rolled marijuana or cannabis
cigarette in the 1950s[34]

---

[34] When I took to Google just now to check the date of the first use
of the word 'joint' meaning a 'cannabis or marijuana cigarette', I was

Liposuction
'Liposuction', also known as 'lipo', is a type of cosmetic surgery that removes fat from the human body; 'lipo' comes from the Greek for 'fat' and has nothing to do with 'lips', into which, these days, people have implants to make them fuller not thinner

Muggles
I could have chosen 'minger' or 'mansplaining', 'memes' or 'metrosexual', 'moobs' or 'mooning', or even have opted for 'miniskirt', the word and fashion that swept the world in the 1960s, but I have gone for 'Muggles', the term for non-magical humans used by J. K. Rowling in her *Harry Potter* books

Nimby
'Not in my back yard'

Obamacare
A health policy promoted by President Obama and an example of a modern phenomenon: linking a set of policies with a person — e.g. Thatcherism and Reaganomics

Pooper-scooper
Very useful. The Sooper Dooper Pooper Scooper was patented in 1956

---

instantly offered three 'dating apps' for cannabis users. The world is not what it was — and 'Google' and 'app' are just two more of the myriad new words my grandparents never knew.

Quidditch
A school game conjured up by J. K. Rowling for her
Harry Potter books

Router
A twenty-first-century piece of computer equipment
that handles signal transfers

Snail-mail
The old-fashioned mail service, which I still use
because so much of my email ends up in the spam
box ... My grandparents would have assumed a 'spam
box' was a tin containing compressed meat

Tangoed
Once those who 'tangoed' were dancers; they still
may be, but if they have overdone the orange
make-up and now look the colour of a bottle
of Tango, they've been tangoed!

Unisex
A 1960s coinage for things (especially clothes and
toilets) designed to be suitable for both sexes

Voicemail
Where you leave your message and I fail to call back

WAGS
Once 'wags' were 'witty chaps'; now they are the
'Wives and Girlfriends', usually of
chaps who play sport

Xbox

'Xbox' is a gaming console brand developed and owned by Microsoft; while my grandparents knew about the 'X factor' (a phrase that's been around since the 1930s), the 'Xbox' would have meant nothing to them; to my grandchildren it means everything

Yogalates

Combining yoga and Pilates

Zonked

Under the influence of drugs or alcohol, or utterly exhausted, or both

It Pays to Increase Your Word Power

It certainly does. Several reliable surveys suggest the larger your vocabulary, the higher your income.

What's the best way to increase your word power? Use the words you already know correctly and with confidence — and add to your vocabulary on a regular basis. How do you do that?

- Go word hunting. Actively search out new, useful, and interesting words. Listen to people who have ways with words that you admire and make a note of the words they use that intrigue, surprise, or impress you. Note down the words, check them out in a dictionary, start slipping them into your own conversation and writing.

- Talk to people from older and younger generations; talk to people from different professions and walks of life; talk to people from different English-speaking countries and different parts of the British Isles. Keep a notebook in which you can record the words you hear that interest you. For example, last week I overheard one of my daughters use a word I'd not heard before. She said she was **hangry** — angry because she was hungry.
- Go dictionary dipping. Find a dictionary, open it at random, and point to a word. If you already know it, great. If you don't, read on, master the word you've found, and then find a way of using it — somehow! anyhow! — within the next twenty-four hours. I collect dictionaries — I have scores of them, ancient and modern — so this is an easy game for me to play. For example, I have just opened my copy of the *Penguin Dictionary of Curious and Interesting Words* and my finger landed on **moil**: verb, 'to churn, to work woefully, to drudge with dread'. You know the feeling?
- Read. Read everything and anything. Read writers who write beautifully: Jane Austen, Virginia Woolf, Elizabeth Taylor. Read writers who do wonderful things with words: Charles Dickens, P. G. Wodehouse, Jonathan Franzen. Read writers outside your usual run of reading. Read poetry. Read song lyrics. Read the rappers. Read the Doncaster Primary Care Health Trust's *Glossary of Yorkshire Medical Terms*. That's where I discovered

that **Barnsley's at home** is a euphemism for 'menstruation' and **sparrow** and **sixpence** euphemisms for the male and female private parts.

- Find back numbers of the *Reader's Digest*, founded in 1920, and for many years the world's best-selling magazine. 'It Pays to Increase Your Word Power' was one of the magazine's most popular and successful features. It was from it that I discovered the word **tergiversate**, meaning 'to be deliberately ambiguous or unclear in order to mislead'. According to *Reader's Digest*, use the verb 'when you need a fancy way to describe someone who's beating around the bush, or being deliberately unclear'. A politician who really doesn't want to answer a reporter's question is likely to **tergiversate**, or talk and talk without ever taking a definitive stand. Your relatives may even **tergiversate** at holiday gatherings when uncomfortable topics come up. The Latin root word, *tergiversari*, literally means 'to turn one's back', or more figuratively, 'to be evasive'.
- Do crosswords. Solve word puzzles. Watch *Countdown* and play along. Play Scrabble — and when you come across a word you don't know (or aren't sure about), check it out and make a note of it in your personal word book.

The best way to remember a new word is to use it. And then use it again. There's no excuse. New research from the department of neurobiology at Columbia University has established that new brain cells grow as quickly when you are in your seventies as when you are in your twenties. Remembering things does not have to get more difficult as you grow older. According to the scientists at Columbia, gradual mental decline 'is not the inevitable process many of us think it is'. The researchers made their discovery after counting the number of new cells growing in the hippocampus, the part of the brain that processes memories and emotions. They found that around 700 brain cells were created each day even in the oldest people they studied, and that there was no difference in the hippocampus in young and old brains.

So, regardless of your age, try to learn a new word every day and test yourself at the end of the week. New to the Brandreth vocabulary this week have been these magnificent seven: **niblings** ('siblings' are your brothers and sisters; 'niblings' are your nephews and nieces); **abecedarian** (someone who is learning the alphabet); **kickie-wickie** (I went to a production of *All's Well That Ends Well* and noticed the word for the first time: it's one of Shakespeare's playful synonyms for 'a wife'); **pingle** (an old verb meaning 'to eat with very little appetite'); **blutter** ('to blurt out'); **woopie** ('a well-off older person'; and **CIO** (an acronym for 'Crying It Out', a method of baby sleep training, as in 'Leave them CIO').

A Scrabble A to Z

I love Scrabble! I come from a family of word-lovers and board-game enthusiasts. In 1936, my father (a lawyer) bought one of the first sets of Monopoly sold in Britain. He met my mother (a teacher) playing Monopoly. After the Second World War, when Scrabble was introduced to

Britain my parents bought one of the first sets to be sold here. In the early 1950s, almost from the age I could walk and talk, I was playing Scrabble. Much of my life-long love of words I owe to this extraordinary game.

When I was thirteen, I was sent to a boarding school called Bedales in Hampshire. The founder of the school, J. H. Badley (1865–1967), lived in the school grounds and on Wednesday afternoons I was sent to play a game of Scrabble with him. He was in his late nineties then and played a mean game. Invariably he won. I told him he was cheating because he used words that were obsolete. He claimed they had been current when he had first learned them. He was a remarkable man. In the 1890s, he knew Oscar Wilde, whose eldest son, Cyril, was a pupil at Bedales. In the 1960s he was playing Scrabble with me. At one hundred, he believed Scrabble kept his mind alive. It did. It does.

By the time I left university, at the beginning of the 1970s, I had become a Scrabble obsessive. I would go so far as to say I had become a Scrabble evangelist: I wanted to spread the word of the world's most wonderful word game. That's how I came to found the National Scrabble Championships in 1971. I was writing a book about prison reform at the time. I had visited Bristol Prison and seen some inmates playing Scrabble. I knew that the Queen played Scrabble. I thought, 'This is a game enjoyed by Her Majesty and those detained at Her Majesty's pleasure: it's a game for everyone. We need a national competition to find the best player in the land.'

From that first national championship, the Scrabble movement grew and grew: competitions proliferated, standards rose, sales soared. We had Scrabble on TV, Scrabble clothes (I had several Scrabble jumpers), Travel Scrabble, computer

Scrabble... You name it, we found a Scrabble angle to it. Yes, there have been and are other enjoyable word games (Bananagrams is another of my favourites), but none can rival Scrabble.

The Association of British Scrabble Players (of which I am the proud president) was formed in 1987 as an organisation to oversee UK tournament Scrabble and its associated rating system. There are now one-day or weekend tournaments somewhere in the British Isles nearly every week, organised by local clubs and individuals, with results rated by the ABSP. Check out www.absp.org.uk to find out more.

Champion Scrabble players have vast vocabularies. My friend Mark Nyman (a former World Champion at Scrabble as well as a former producer at *Countdown*), has an encyclopaedic knowledge of the words that are allowable in Scrabble. Many of them are pretty obscure. Many of them are abbreviations or foreign words that have crept into the Scrabble dictionary because they are so useful to the game. I knew that **qi** is allowed in Scrabble as an alternative spelling of **chi**, meaning the 'life force' in Chinese philosophy and medicine; I knew that **zo** is an approved Scrabble word because it's one way of spelling the word for a type of Himalayan cattle; but I have only just discovered from Mark Nyman that **za** is permissible, as a colloquial abbreviation for 'pizza'.

With a little help from my friend, here is my A to Z of useful and unusual words to play at Scrabble:

aa
volcanic lava

azulejo
a Spanish porcelain tile

274

bambi

born again middle-aged biker

boobird

someone who boos

caz

short for 'casual'

cineaste

film enthusiast

dweebish

quite stupid

divi

very stupid

ee

eye

elint

electronic intelligence

fetology

study of the foetus

fjeld

a high rocky Scandinavian plateau

gosht
an Indian meat dish

gymp
to limp

hili
a scar on a seed

huhu
a hairy New Zealand beetle

io
a moth

icekhana
a race on a frozen lake

jerepigo
a sweet fortified wine

jube
a gallery in a church

kaal
an Afrikaans word for 'naked'

koha
a Maori gift

luz
an indestructible human bone

lunkhead
a stupid person

maxed
reached full extent

mips
million instructions per second

nox
nitrogen oxide

nonwords
yes, 'nonwords' meaning 'nonwords' is allowed!

oi
a shout for attention

oreades
mountain nymphs

pht
a sound to express irritation

patootie
a backside

qin
a Chinese musical instrument

qwerty
a keyboard

ritornel
an orchestral passage

rodney
a small Canadian fishing boat

slyboots
a sly one

sweetman
a Caribbean man kept by a woman

tiglic
a syrup liquid

tiz
a state of confusion

ubique
everywhere

ulva
seaweed

veep
vice-president

waugh
to bark

whump
to make a dull thud

xerafin
an Indian coin

xerotic
abnormal dryness of bodily tissues
(some words just don't live up to their promise)

yahooism
crude behaviour

yuzu
a citrus fruit

zit
a pimple

zzzs
sleeps
(they allow 'zzz' for a sleep in Scrabble, so they have to
allow 'zzzs'. I know, I know, but it's only a game)

10. The Rules

According to the nineteenth-century American writer and publisher Elbert Hubbard: 'Grammar is the grave of letters.' He might be right, but who is reading Elbert Hubbard now?

Sticking rigidly to the rules certainly isn't the secret of good writing, but I believe knowing the rules before you decide to abandon them is important.

According to Stephen King (and a lot of people are reading him now): 'If you don't have time to read, you don't have the time (or the tools) to write. Simple as that.' In the 1890s, Rudyard Kipling (as popular then as Stephen King is now) gave this advice to a young woman who was thinking of becoming a writer: 'Copy the great for craftsmanship, write as much as you can like Dickens, imitate Henry James, study Thackeray. Out of all this you will evolve a style of your own. Only, write! write! write! and — WORK!' When the young woman showed him a story she had written, he crossed out the word 'partake', marking it as 'vile oh vile', and 'scorned such expressions as "blue ether", "rugged features", "pointing with disdain" and other journalese'.

I am not sure that the American novelist Elmore Leonard would have approved of all those exclamations in Kipling's letter. He advised writers: 'Keep your exclamation points under control. You are allowed no more than two or three per 100,000 words of prose.' Stephen King says: 'The road to hell is paved with adverbs.' The great advertising man of the twentieth century, David Ogilvy, counselled: 'Never use jargon words like *reconceptualise*, *demassification*, *attitudinally*, *judgmentally*. They are hallmarks of a pretentious ass.'

'Write drunk, edit sober,' said Ernest Hemingway — which is a problem for me because I don't drink alcohol. I don't drink coffee, either. And I've given up meat and fish. I'm simply dedicating my remaining years to hunting down misplaced apostrophes and doing what I can to improve spelling among the young.

This is not meant to be a book about fine writing, but before I go I am sharing advice from some fine writers with you because the best writers are wonderful communicators and good communication *is* what this book is meant to be about.

George Orwell's Rules

Here are six rules from the great George Orwell, first published in *Horizon* magazine in 1946. They still apply now.

1. Never use a metaphor, simile or other figure of speech which you are used to seeing in print.
2. Never use a long word where a short one will do.
3. If it is possible to cut a word out, always cut it out.
4. Never use the passive where you can use the active.

5. Never use a foreign phrase, a scientific word or a jargon word if you can think of an everyday English equivalent.
6. Break any of these rules sooner than say anything outright barbarous.

The Martin Amis Rules

Martin Amis is another fine writer. His memoir, *Experience*, is one of my favourite books. He was the Professor of Creative Writing at the Centre for New Writing at the University of Manchester for several years and these are his 'rules' for writers. I don't follow them all — e.g. I do set myself a daily word target and I'm partial to a punning title — but Martin Amis has won rather more literary prizes than I have, so read on and take note.

1. Write in long-hand: when you scratch out a word, it still exists there on the page. On the computer, when you delete a word it disappears for ever. This is important because usually your first instinct is the right one.
2. Minimum number of words to write every day: no 'quota'. Sometimes it will be no words. Sometimes it will be 1500.
3. Use any anxiety you have about your writing — or your life – as fuel: Ambition and anxiety: that's the writer's life.
4. Never say 'sci-fi.' You'll enrage purists. Call it SF.

5. Don't dumb down: always write for your top five per cent of readers.
6. Never pun your title, simpler is usually better: *Lolita* turns out to be a great title; couldn't be simpler.
7. At Manchester my rule is I don't look at their work. We read great books, and we talk about them … We look at Conrad, Dostoyevsky.
8. When is an idea worth pursuing in novel-form? It's got to give you a kind of glimmer.
9. Watch out for words that repeat too often.
10. Don't start a paragraph with the same word as the previous one. That goes doubly for sentences.
11. Stay in the tense.
12. Inspect your 'hads' and see if you really need them.
13. Never use 'amongst.' Never use 'whilst.' Anyone who uses 'whilst' is subliterate.
14. Try not to write sentences that absolutely anyone could write.
15. You write the book you want to read. That's my rule.
16. You have to have a huge appetite for solitude.

The William Safire Rules

Years ago, in the US, I had a syndicated column about words and language called 'Alphabet Soup', and, because of it, began to correspond with William Safire (1929–2009), presidential speech writer, *New York Times* columnist, and celebrated word buff, who sent me the amusing 'rules for writers' he had devised and collected over the years.

1. Remember to never split an infinitive.
2. The passive voice should never be used.
3. Do not put statements in the negative form.
4. Don't use no double negatives.
5. Verbs has to agree with their subjects.
6. Proofread carefully to see if you words out.
7. If you reread your work, you can find on rereading a great deal of repetition can be avoided by rereading and editing.
8. A writer must not shift your point of view.
9. And don't start a sentence with a conjunction.
10. Don't overuse exclamation marks!!
11. Place pronouns as close as possible, especially in long sentences, as of 10 or more words, to their antecedents.
12. Writing carefully, dangling participles must be avoided.
13. If any word is improper at the end of a sentence, a linking verb is.
14. Take the bull by the hand and avoid mixing metaphors.
15. Avoid trendy locutions that sound flaky.
16. Always pick on the correct idiom.
17. The adverb always follows the verb.
18. Never use a preposition to end a sentence with.
19. Avoid annoying alliteration.
20. Don't verb nouns.

21. Make each pronoun agree with their antecedent.
22. Don't use commas, which aren't necessary.
23. About those sentence fragments.
24. Its important to use apostrophe's correctly.
25. Correct spelling is esential.
26. Between you and I, case is important.
27. Last but not least, avoid clichés like the plague; seek viable alternatives.

The Gyles Brandreth Rules

I don't go along with all the Safire Rules. In my book, you can split the occasional infinitive. 'To boldly go' — why not? And you can start a sentence with a conjunction now and again. Safire is right about 'verbing' nouns (I cannot bear all that 'medalling' at the Olympic Games), and right, too, to give a big no-no to double negatives, though once in a while they can serve a purpose. 'I didn't do nothing right' is clearly wrong — but 'I wouldn't say I don't like you' is a double negative trying to tell us something quite subtle. No, I don't knock no double negatives. And don't you knock them either. 'I Can't Get No Satisfaction' has made Mick Jagger and Keith Richards many millions since its release in 1965.

English is the richest language in the world — and it's evolving all the time. Words will come and go, and the rules of grammar can't be set in stone. Good English is all about good communication: saying, writing, texting, tweeting, emailing what you want to say as clearly as you can. Remember my five 'A's:

Be **accurate**

- It helps: inaccuracy causes confusion

Be **ambitious**

- It pays to increase your word power

Be **adventurous**

- Dare to be different in the words you use and the way in which you use them

Be **accepting**

- Language will change and not every change is for the worse

Be **aware**

- Think about what you say and how it will be received and understood by others

And finally...

You must remember this: a kiss is just a kiss ...

You need words to say 'I love you'. Words are everything. And the more accurately and effectively you use words in this world, the more successful and the happier you will be. Enough said.

Postscript
The Language of Grammar

sentence

noun

1. A set of words that is complete in itself, typically containing a subject and predicate, conveying a statement, question, exclamation, or command, and consisting of a main clause and sometimes one or more subordinate clauses.
2. The punishment assigned to a defendant found guilty by a court, or fixed by law for a particular offence.

Sentence, noun, subject, predicate, main clause, subordinate clauses, verb…

Aaargh!

What's this all about? Do I need to know?

I am not sure you do, which is why I'm tucking this away at the back of the book, so that those who regard a lesson in grammar as the worst kind of punishment can skip this bit. In the French playwright Molière's famous play, *Le bourgeois gentilhomme*, Monsieur Jourdain is thrilled to discover that he has been 'speaking prose' all his life without realising it. You have been using grammar since you learned to speak and read and write, without necessarily knowing the names of all the parts of speech or understanding what they are supposed to do. I have been driving a car for forty years without looking inside the engine once. I couldn't tell you the difference between a camshaft and a crankcase, but I am glad they're there.

In case you do want to know more about the language of grammar, read on. And let's start with a **sentence** as in '*noun* 1' above. That definition, I hope, is clear enough.

A **sentence** often features a **verb.** The **verb** is the action or 'doing' word. The person or thing doing the action is the **subject** of the **sentence**. The subject is either a **noun** or a **pronoun**. If the action is being done to someone or something, that is the **object** of the **sentence** and is also a **noun** or a **pronoun**.

The **predicate** is the part of a **sentence** containing a verb and stating something about the **subject** (e.g. 'banging on a bit', as in: 'Gyles is banging on a bit.') A **clause** is part of a **sentence** and contains a **subject** and a **verb**. 'Gyles writes books and people sometimes read them' is a **sentence** with two **main clauses** ('Gyles writes books' and 'people sometimes read them'), so called because they are each of equal importance and could exist as separate sentences.

A **subordinate clause** contains a **subject** and a **verb**, but it needs to be attached to a **main clause** because it cannot make sense on its own. 'Gyles writes about grammar with a damp towel wrapped around his head' is a

sentence with a **main clause** ('Gyles writes about grammar') and a **subordinate clause** ('with a damp towel wrapped around his head').

A **common noun** is a **noun** that refers to people, places, and things in general. A **proper noun** identifies a particular person, place, or thing, e.g. 'Gyles' in 'London' in 'January' (three proper nouns) with 'a headache', 'a cold', and 'a conscience' (three common nouns).

A **concrete noun** is a noun which refers to people and to things that exist physically and can be seen, touched, smelled, heard, or tasted, e.g. the 'coffee', 'biscuits', and 'cake' 'Gyles' is resorting to right now. An **abstract noun** refers to ideas, qualities, and conditions which have no physical reality, e.g. Gyles's 'hope' that you are still reading this and his 'anguish' if you aren't.

Collective nouns refer to groups of people or things, e.g. 'family', 'flock', 'government', 'herd', 'team'. In American English, most collective nouns are treated as singular, with a singular verb, e.g. 'The whole family was in uproar.' In British English, while that sentence would be correct, it is also correct to treat the collective noun as a plural, with a plural verb, e.g. 'The whole family were in despair.'

A noun may belong to more than one category, e.g. 'despair' is both a **common noun** and an **abstract noun**, and 'Gyles' is both a both a **concrete noun** and a **proper noun**.

A **pronoun** is used in place of a noun to avoid repetition. **Personal pronouns** are used in place of nouns referring to specific people or things. The **personal pronouns** 'I', 'you', 'we', 'he', 'she', 'it', and 'they' are known as **subjective pronouns** because they act as the subjects of verbs — e.g. 'I met

Gyles.' The **personal pronouns** 'me', 'you', 'us', 'him', 'her', 'it', and 'them' are called **objective pronouns** because they act as the objects of verbs — e.g. 'Gyles liked me.' The **personal pronouns** 'mine', 'yours', 'hers', 'his', 'ours', and 'theirs' are known as **possessive pronouns** because they refer to something owned by the speaker or by someone or something previously mentioned. **Reflexive personal pronouns** include 'myself', 'himself', 'herself', 'itself', 'ourselves', 'yourselves', and 'themselves'. They are used to refer back to the subject of the **clause** in which they are used — e.g. 'I read on and surprised myself.'

Relative pronouns introduce **relative clauses**. The most common relative pronouns are 'who', 'whom', 'whose', 'which', and 'that'. 'Who' refers to people and sometimes pet animals; 'which' refers to animals and things; 'that' refers to people, animals, and things. 'Whose' is possessive and used for people and animals, and sometimes (if controversially) for things. We debated the debatable value of 'whom' back on page 195.

A **preposition** is used before a **noun** or **pronoun** to indicate place (e.g. 'above', 'below', 'beside', 'behind'), position ('on', 'under', 'into', 'by') or time ('until', 'since', 'after').

Conjunctions join together two words, two phrases, or two parts of a sentence. The twenty-five most common conjunctions are: 'and', 'that', 'but', 'or', 'as', 'if', 'when', 'than', 'because', 'while', 'where', 'after', 'so', 'though', 'since', 'until', 'whether', 'before', 'although', 'nor', 'like', 'once', 'unless', 'now', and 'except'.

An **adjective** is a word that describes a **noun**, giving extra information about it. A **descriptive adjective** is just that — e.g. 'handsome', 'happy', 'hysterical', 'grey', 'green'. A quantitative adjective is just that — e.g. 'some', 'all', 'both', 'many', 'ten'. An adjective can be **positive**, **comparative**, or **superlative** — e.g. 'tall', 'taller', 'tallest'; 'small', 'smaller', 'smallest'. The '-er' and '-est' suffixes don't apply with every adjective — e.g. 'bad', 'worse', 'worst'. With adjectives of more than one syllable, as a rule, 'more' and 'most' are used with the **positive adjective** to give the **comparative** and **superlative** — e.g. 'more beautiful' and 'most beautiful' instead of 'beautifuller' and 'beautifullest'.

Verbs are the 'doing' words. **Transitive verbs** need an object; **intransitive verbs** don't. 'To give', 'to do', 'to make', 'to find' are **transitive verbs**. 'To hope', 'to speak', 'to laugh', 'to cry', aren't. Many verbs can be both **transitive** and **intransitive**. 'Gyles sings in the shower' is **intransitive**. 'Gyles sings his favourite song' is **transitive**.

Depending on the way in which you word a **sentence**, a **verb** can be either **active** or **passive**. When the verb is **active**, the **subject** of the **verb** is doing the action — e.g. 'Gyles swept all before him.' When the **verb** is **passive**, the subject undergoes the action rather than doing it—e.g. 'Gyles was reduced to tears.' As a rule, the **active** voice is more effective than the **passive** — e.g. 'I have nothing to offer but blood, toil, tears and sweat' is **active** and more effective than 'Blood, toil, tears and sweat are what's on offer.'

Auxiliary verbs help form the various **tenses** of other verbs. The principal ones are 'be', 'do', and 'have'. The **tense** of a verb tells you when a person did something or when something existed or happened. In English, there are three main tenses: the **present**, the **past**, and the **future**.

The **present tense** (e.g. 'I write') is also called the **present simple**. The **past tense** (e.g. 'I wrote') is also called the **past**

simple. The **future tense** (e.g. 'I will write' or 'I shall write') is used to refer to things that haven't yet happened.

There are two further types of tense: the **continuous** and the **perfect**. **Continuous tenses** are used to talk about actions that continue for a period of time. They are formed with the relevant **tense** of the **auxiliary verb** 'to be' and the **present participle** of the **main verb**. A **participle** is a word formed from a **verb** (e.g. 'writing') and used as an **adjective** (e.g. 'writing machine') or a **noun** (e.g. 'fine writing'). **Participle**s are also used to make **compound verb** forms (e.g. 'is writing', 'has written'). There are three main continuous tenses: the **present continuous** ('I am writing'); the **past continuous** ('I was writing'); the **future continuous** ('I will be writing').

Perfect tenses are used to talk about actions that are completed by the present or a particular point in the past or future. They are formed with the relevant **tense** of the **auxiliary verb** 'to have' and the **past participle** of the main verb. There are three main perfect tenses: the **present perfect** ('I have written'); the **past perfect** ('I had written'); and the **future perfect** ('I will have written').

The **present perfect continuous** ('I have been working') is used to talk about how long something has continued up until now; the **past perfect continuous** ('I had been working') is used to talk about something which continued up to a particular moment in the past but is now completed; and the **future perfect continuous** ('I will have been writing') is used to talk about something which is expected to end by a particular time in the future.

Sometimes an **auxiliary verb** is used with a **participle** in the **present** and **past tenses** — e.g. 'I am writing', 'I have written'. **Conditional tenses** involve possibilities — e.g. 'I would write a love poem if you smiled at me'; 'I could write a love poem if I was in the mood'; 'I should write a love poem if I hope to be immortal'.

Groucho Marx is the celebrated master of the **dangling participle** and **misplaced modifier**. In the 1930 film *Animal Crackers*, Marx — as the character Captain Spaulding — gives an account of his adventures in Africa: 'One morning I shot an elephant in my pyjamas. How he got in my pyjamas I don't know.'

The **dangling participle** or **misplaced modifier** is a phrase — often used at the beginning of a sentence — that modifies the **subject** of the **sentence** in a way that leaves the meaning ambiguous — e.g. 'Flying over the African landscape, the elephant herd looked magnificent', or 'Covered in hot chocolate sauce, we devoured the ice cream sundae'.

An **adverb** is a word used to give information about a **verb, adjective,** or other **adverb. Adverb** means 'added word' and **adverbs** fall into three categories telling us when ('sometime', 'soon', 'now', 'never', etc.) or where ('somewhere', 'here', 'beside', 'along', etc.) or how something happened ('simply', 'excitedly', 'hopelessly', 'swiftly', etc.). The 'how' **adverbs** are usually formed by adding '-ly' to the **adjective. Adverbs** can make the meaning of a **verb, adjective,** or other **adverb** stronger or weaker, and often appear between the subject and its verb (e.g. 'He nearly lost everything' — which is not the same thing, of course, as 'He lost nearly everything'). Many **adverbs, adjectives,** and **prepositions** are the same words. What they are called depends on their position and function in a sentence.

A **preposition** is a word such as 'after', 'across', 'beyond', 'in', 'to', 'on', 'up', 'underneath', 'with'. **Prepositions** are usually used in front of **nouns** or **pronouns** and they show the relationship between the **noun** or **pronoun** and other words in a **sentence**. They describe, for example, the position of something, the time when something happens, or the way in which something is done.

Because a **preposition** usually comes before a noun ('pre-position' — get it?) it is often said you should not end a sentence with a preposition. Not so. Legend among lexicographers has it Winston Churchill pointed out the absurdity of the idea when he said, 'This is the sort of English up with which I will not put.' Put the preposition where it falls naturally. Some of the stuff you learned at school may no longer apply. Don't be taken in.

A **determiner** is a word that introduces a noun and limits its meaning — e.g. 'the', 'a', 'an', 'every', 'this', 'those', 'my', 'whose, 'five', etc. The determiner 'the' is also known as the **definite article** and the **determiner** 'a' or 'an' as the **indefinite article**.

An **exclamation**, also called an **interjection**, is a word or phrase that expresses emotion, such as surprise, delight, or anger. Exclamations often stand on their own, and in writing they are usually followed by an exclamation mark rather than a full stop.

Aaargh!

(where we came in) is a good example.

Acknowledgements and Further Reading

I am indebted to my parents who first gave me my love of language. I am very grateful, too, to the teachers who taught me English at school, especially to Mr Gardiner, the head of English at Bedales when I was a pupil there in the 1960s. (If you want to find out how important he was to me, he features prominently in my published diaries: *Something Sensational to Read in the Train*.) I am grateful to all the friends I have made over the years, playing Scrabble and taking part in *Countdown*, including, among others, Mark Nyman, Olive Behan, Anne Bradford, Philip Nelkon, Darryl Francis, Damian Eadie, Nick Hewer, and, of course, the *doyenne* of Dictionary Corner, Susie Dent. I am grateful, also, to my scholarly friends at the Queen's English Society, notably to the president, Dr Bernard C. Lamb, and the former membership secretary, Michael Plumbe. If you want to know more about the Society, take at look at the website: queens-english-society.org. Prior to publication, I have not shared any part of my book with any of the above, so that any errors are my responsibility and the opinions I have expressed are entirely my own.

I am very grateful to my agent, Jonathan Lloyd at Curtis Brown, and my publisher, Dan Bunyard at Michael Joseph, for making the book happen, and to the team at Michael Joseph — Lucy Beresford-Knox, Beth Cockeram, Sam Deacon, Louise Jones, Amy McWalters, Alice Mottram and

Chris Turner among them — for making it happen so happily. Over excellent sandwiches, Beatrix McIntyre and I did our best to resolve all the queries raised by my redoubtable copy-editor, Kit Shepherd, and I thank him and her (and Bogdan in the Penguin catering department) for their contribution to our joint endeavour. I would also like to thank my indexer, Caroline Wilding.

Years ago, I was lucky enough to be befriended by Dr Robert Burchfield, a delightful New Zealander, lexicographer, scholar, and writer, who edited the *Oxford English Dictionary* for thirty years to 1986. He gave me the complete *Oxford English Dictionary* (all fourteen volumes) when I was in my twenties. Since then, I have acquired scores of other dictionaries and hundreds of assorted books about words. I have not read all of them, so this reading list is by no means comprehensive. But if you have enjoyed *Have You Eaten Grandma?* you might also enjoy some of these.

Gyles Brandreth, *The Joy of Lex: An Amazing and Amusing Z to A and A to Z of Words*, 1987

Gyles Brandreth, *The 7 Secrets of Happiness: An Optimist's Journey*, 2013

Gyles Brandreth, *Word Play: A Cornucopia of Puns, Anagrams, Euphemisms and Other Contortions and Curiosities of the English Language*, 2015

Michèle Brown, *Break a Leg: A Dictionary of Theatrical Quotations*, 2018

R. W. Burchfield, *The New Fowler's Modern English Usage*, revised edition, 1998

Susie Dent, *Dent's Modern Tribes: The Secret Languages of Britain*, 2016

Susie Dent, *Susie Dent's Weird Words*, 2013

Matthew Engel, *That's the Way It Crumbles: The American Conquest of the English Language*, 2017

Emmy J. Favilla, *A World Without "Whom": The Essential Guide to Language in the BuzzFeed Age*, 2017

H. W. Fowler and F. G. Fowler, *The King's English*, third edition, 1930

Ernest Gowers, *Plain Words: A Guide to the Use of English*, 1948

Rebecca Gowers, *Horrible Words: A Guide to the Misuse of English*, 2016

Paul Anthony Jones, *Word Drops: A Sprinkling of Linguistic Curiosities*, 2015

Bernard C. Lamb, *The Queen's English and How to Use It*, 2010

Noah Lukeman, *The Art of Punctuation*, 2006

Mark Nyman, *Collins Little Book of Scrabble Secrets*, 2016

Dorothy Paull, *The Ladybird Book of Spelling and Grammar*, 1984

George Stone Saussy III, *The Penguin Dictionary of Curious and Interesting Words*, 1986

Caroline Taggart and J. A. Wines, *My Grammar and I (or Should That Be 'Me'?): Old-School Ways to Sharpen Your English*, 2008

Lynne Truss, *Eats, Shoots & Leaves: The Zero Tolerance Approach to Punctuation*, 2003

Richard Whiteley, *Letters Play! A Treasury of Words and Wordplay*, 1995

Index